BEAUTIFUL KINGDOM

A DELIGHT MINISTRIES STUDY

MOMENTS FROM THE BOOK OF MATTHEW

Copyright © by Delight Ministries
All Rights Reserved
Book design by Hailey Sheppard
Theological Editing by Aubrey Johnston
Editing by Maddie Grimes

No part of this book may be reproduced in any form or by any electronic or mechanical means including information storage and retrieval systems, without permission in writing from Delight Ministries.

All Scripture quotations, unless otherwise indicated, are taken from the Holy Bible, New International Version®, NIV®. Copyright ©1973, 1978, 1984, 2011 by Biblica, Inc.™ Used by permission of Zondervan. All rights reserved worldwide. www.zondervan.com The "NIV" and "New International Version" are trademarks registered in the United States Patent and Trademark Office by Biblica, Inc.™

Delight Ministries
www.delightministries.com

Printed in the United States of America
First Printing: January 2024
Color House Graphics
ISBN: 978-1-7343272-8-1

Our Mission

Our mission is to invite college women into **Christ-centered community** that **fosters vulnerability** and **transforms stories.**

CHRIST-CENTERED COMMUNITY

We launch, grow, and sustain thriving Christ-centered communities on college campuses. We've seen time and time again that community is often the catalyst for true Kingdom impact.

FOSTER VULNERABILITY

We aim to provide a space on college campuses for women to vulnerably share how Christ has been at work in their lives. We believe that vulnerability leads to breakthrough, and breakthrough leads to transformation!

TRANSFORMS STORIES

We believe that one moment with Jesus can truly change everything. Our mission is to give college women numerous opportunities to meet with Jesus and have their lives transformed!

TABLE OF CONTENTS

CHAPTER 1
BEAUTIFUL KINGDOM
/ PAGE 18

CHAPTER 2
HOW TO PRAY
/ PAGE 38

CHAPTER 3
FIRST THINGS FIRST
/ PAGE 56

CHAPTER 4
JESUS AND MESSY PEOPLE
/ PAGE 72

CHAPTER 5
COME TO ME
/ PAGE 90

CHAPTER 6
WHEN JESUS CALLS YOU OUT
/ PAGE 108

CHAPTER 7
GLORY
/ PAGE 126

CHAPTER 8
FOR THE LEAST OF THESE
/ PAGE 144

CHAPTER 9
BEAUTIFUL TRUST
/ PAGE 164

CHAPTER 10
WOMEN ON MISSION
/ PAGE 182

HOW TO READ THIS BOOK

SCRIPTURE

In this study, we'll be walking through the Gospel of Matthew. This is such an amazing book of the Bible full of important moments, so we won't be able to cover everything. Instead of a verse-by-verse breakdown of the entire Gospel, you can think of this study as an exploration. We're cruising through the text and pulling out specific moments we feel called to focus on for this study; moments where we see the *Beautiful Kingdom* come to life. If you want to read the parts we weren't able to cover on your own time, we totally recommend it!

Each week you'll be reading anywhere from a few verses to a few chapters of Matthew as we work our way through the book. The chapters in this study will walk you through the reading process. As you read, you'll answer questions, fill in the blanks, and hopefully get a deeper understanding of the context behind what you're reading. You'll want to pull out your Bible and start reading anytime you see something like this...

Read Matthew 1:1-17.

Just remember that this is your cue to pause and open the Word. Please don't skip reading the actual Word of God! We promise that our words pale in comparison to what God can say to you directly through Scripture!

Primarily, we will use the NIV translation when citing Scripture throughout this study. Feel free to use whatever translation works for you, but you might be a tad confused on some of the fill-in-the-blanks if you use a different Bible translation. You can always head to BibleGateway.com to access a free version of the NIV if you need it.

Each week, we will zero in on a topic that the Scripture introduces, using three main points to guide our journey through the text. Our prayer is that this book brings new light to Bible stories and verses that you've perhaps read a million times.

THINK IT THROUGH
You'll notice that all throughout the book, we ask you questions under the title "Think it through." These questions are your opportunity to take it deeper, to do some personal reflection and allow the Scripture to begin to soak into your heart and life. These are moments of evaluating where you're at and embracing the hard truth. Don't just answer how you think you should answer; answer as honestly as possible! There is such freedom to be found when we come before the Lord with all of our mess and imperfections! We promise that as you get vulnerable before the Lord, He will unlock even deeper intimacy.

STOP AND PRAY
In each chapter you will find a "stop and pray" opportunity. These are invitations to take a moment to open your heart up to the Lord and welcome Him into your reading. You can pray them out loud, rewrite them in your journal, or simply sit and let the words soak in. Whatever you do, don't miss these moments to center your heart and connect with the Lord!

CONVERSATION STARTERS
Our goal is to get the conversation rolling between you and the Lord, within your Delight community, or through a small group! These questions found at the end of every chapter will help you do just that. We suggest setting some time aside each week to think through your answers to these questions in a prayerful way with the Lord. Then, come ready to discuss them with whoever you're processing this study with. We promise that the more time you take to prepare on the front end, the better your conversations will be!

TAKE YOUR TIME
Remember that you have an entire week to get through each chapter! Don't feel like you have to do it all in one sitting. Take your time with it and try to process and understand every last verse. There's no pressure to get through an entire chapter in one day. Break up the content however works best for you!

TIPS FOR READING SCRIPTURE

The truth is, reading Scripture isn't always easy! It's a muscle that you have to stretch and grow over time. We've compiled a list of tips from some of our friends that will help you to start to love your daily time in the Word. These are all practical tips that will help you to better hear the voice of God through the Scripture.

#1 PREPARE YOUR HEART – This is SO simple! Every day before you open the Word, ask God to simply prepare your heart, show up, and speak to you. Reading the Bible isn't something we have to do on our own or through our own power. The Word is alive, meaning that God can and will speak to you through it. All you have to do is ask!

#2 ASK GOOD QUESTIONS – This can seriously change the way you encounter the Bible! The best tool we have to understand the Word of God is our ability to ask the right questions. If you've ever read Scripture and not understood something (a.k.a. us every day of our lives), that's an invitation to ask a question. What? When? How? Where? Who? Why? Dig into your questions and seek out answers!

For some of your more historical or practical questions, you can read biblical commentaries, get a study Bible, or talk to someone you trust with more biblical knowledge or Bible study experience. For the other more complex questions, bring them to the feet of Jesus and simply ask. He cares and can provide answers in some of the coolest ways! This isn't your college calculus class where you have to be afraid of looking stupid. There is a loving, caring, and gentle Father on the other end of the line ready to have dialogue with you.

If this is new to you . . . don't worry! We're going to ask A LOT of questions about the text together in this book.

#3 READ AT YOUR OWN PACE – Take your time with reading Scripture! You have your entire life to read the Bible. If you want to meditate on one verse for an entire week, do it! If you want to read the entire Bible in a month, do that! Go at the pace that feels comfortable to you. Don't be afraid to slow down and dive really deep in certain parts when you feel led to.

#4 TALK ABOUT IT – Some of the best moments of revelation from Scripture happen by simply talking about the things you've been reading. This isn't a journey you have to travel alone! Be sure to talk about how God is speaking to you through His Word with your roommate, friends, parents, and your Delight community!

#5 FOLLOW THE SPIRIT – When you're reading your Bible, don't be afraid to change course from where you initially started. You may start out reading Genesis but then feel a nudge to reread that Psalm you heard the other day. Don't ignore those nudges! When you open up your heart to hear from the Lord, He may redirect you to another passage of Scripture. And that is absolutely OK. You never know what He might be leading you to.

BEFORE WE BEGIN

This summer, I did a Bible shred with some of my friends in Delight. Now, if you don't know what a Bible shred is, it's where you set aside a certain amount of days (in our case 60) in which you plan to read the entire Bible.

Yup, that's sixty-six books in sixty days. Sounds intimidating, right?

It was *wild*. Half of my friends dropped out in Genesis, and I switched to listening to the Scripture read out loud on 2x speed by week three. I trudged through Leviticus, celebrated when I got to Psalms, and then, when I finally got to the last two chapters of Revelation, I gave up.

Two chapters away from reading the entire Bible, I quit. My husband was appalled, and I, embarrassed, neglected to tell any of my friends that I never actually finished.

You see, I went into the shred over-confident. I love to read and I love the Bible, so I thought it would be easy to just crank it out. Twenty chapters a day? No problem! I can read a cheesy romance novel in an evening. Certainly this would be a better use of my time, right? And on top of that, I even judged my friends who dropped out early. *Why can't they do it?* I wondered. *It's not that hard!*

But, the further I got into it, the more it started to feel like drudgery. Every waking minute was consumed with the numbers—how many chapters I had left to read that day and how many I should factor in to make up for what I missed the day before when I fell asleep too early. And, as proud of myself as I was for sticking it out, I began to feel like something was missing. Something big and important.

For most of my adult life, I had committed to spending dedicated time with the Lord every day. I grew to depend on that quiet time in the morning with my candle lit and my journal open, engaging in a two-way conversation with God. Sometimes I would list out my feelings and let Him speak into them, sometimes I would read a daily devotional that pointed me to a certain moment in Scripture, and sometimes I would sing the Psalms out loud, allowing His Word to sink into my bones when I was desperate for it. It was communion with God, quality time with my Maker and lover of my soul.

That's what my heart grew to crave during my two months of frantic reading: *intimacy*. In my hurry to read as much Scripture as I possibly could, I inadvertently put myself on a two-month fast from the presence of the very God I was so eager to learn about. I was like a baby who tried to switch to solid foods when my stomach was only ready for milk; I was looking for sustenance but missing the nutrients God was offering me with open hands.

The moment that realization hit, I stopped shredding. Two chapters away from achieving the goal I had planned to brag about for years, I quit. And the next day, in the quiet hours of the morning, I sat down and prayed. *Lord, I just want to be with you.*

> **"ONE THING I ASK FROM THE LORD, THIS ONLY DO I SEEK: THAT I MAY DWELL IN THE HOUSE OF THE LORD ALL THE DAYS OF MY LIFE, TO GAZE ON THE BEAUTY OF THE LORD AND TO SEEK HIM IN HIS TEMPLE."**
> **Psalm 27:4**

Reading your Bible is critical. It's a must-do as a child of God. Scripture is a beautiful gift from the King Himself, a front-row seat to His character and His heart. By no means am I telling you to skip your Bible reading because it's pointless. In fact, I'm not even telling you Bible shreds are bad because I actually believe that reading the whole Bible in order offers a beautiful image of the grand story God has been forming throughout the history of the world.

But I am saying this: we can do nothing apart from Him. Trying to read our Bibles the same way we read our textbooks is bound to leave us feeling frustrated, overextended, and burnt out. Because we aren't called to read just to learn historical facts or just to say we've read the whole Bible. When we read the Bible, we are entering into intimacy with the Father. We're engaging in a conversation with the One who wrote it. The Holy Spirit inside of us is whispering over our shoulder, molding and forming us as we take little bites of the best kind of sustenance.

When was the last time you simply sat and gazed at the beauty of the Lord? Do you crave to dwell in the presence of God, just as it says in Psalm 27:4? If it's been a while—or even if you've never experienced that kind of intimacy with God—that's OK. That's why we wrote this book. Our study of the book of Matthew, *Beautiful Kingdom*, is an invitation to do just that: to sit at the feet of our Savior and marvel at His beauty.

We're going to walk through the book of Matthew and find the beauty in the Kingdom of Heaven that Jesus came to earth to announce. There's no pressure to know every fact and figure about this Gospel, and there's no expectation that by the end you'll be able to quote the whole book from memory. In fact, we can think of this study as sort of the opposite of that frantic Bible shred I tried this summer. We're just toddlers holding onto the hand of our friend Jesus as He walks us through His Word and tells us about His life on earth and His plans for His Kingdom.

We have one goal for this study. It's that by the end, you would be able to step into the presence of God and say, *Jesus you're beautiful*.

Are you ready? Let's step into a new kind of intimacy, together.

**XOXO,
Maggie Sawler**
DELIGHT MINISTRIES
CURRICULUM DEVELOPMENT COORDINATOR

BEAUTIFUL KINGDOM

CHAPTER 1

BEAUTIFUL KINGDOM

Matthew 3

"Attention-grabbing intro."

That's what I had written in my notes to kick off this book. I wanted to start chapter 1 off with a bang—something to spark your interest and get you fired up about diving into a new study, something to make you want to run to your Bible and fling it open to Matthew and read like your life depends on it.

I brainstormed quirky stories, deep and thought-provoking metaphors, and tear-jerking observations about life. But I have to be honest with you . . . It just didn't feel right. Everything I came up with felt empty. But maybe God's trying to teach me

01 / BEAUTIFUL KINGDOM

something—to teach us all something. Maybe we don't have to add flowery language and bells and whistles to His Word to make it attractive. Don't get me wrong, He loves our creativity and He loves when we use our gifts for His glory. But somewhere along the way, is it possible we've started to think His Word isn't enough?

It's hitting me hard right now, staring at my computer and asking God to give me the words. And the answer is so simple: *He already did*.

Here at Delight, we believe in the power of God's Word in Scripture. We believe it's living and active (Hebrews 4:12), and we believe it never returns empty (Isaiah 55:11). So that's where we're going to start: in His Word. *God* will grab your attention. *God* will tug on your heartstrings. *God* will give you a burning desire to read your Bible.

So let's open it up.

+ FLIP TO MATTHEW 1:1 AND COPY IT DOWN IN THE SPACE BELOW.

BEAUTIFUL KINGDOM

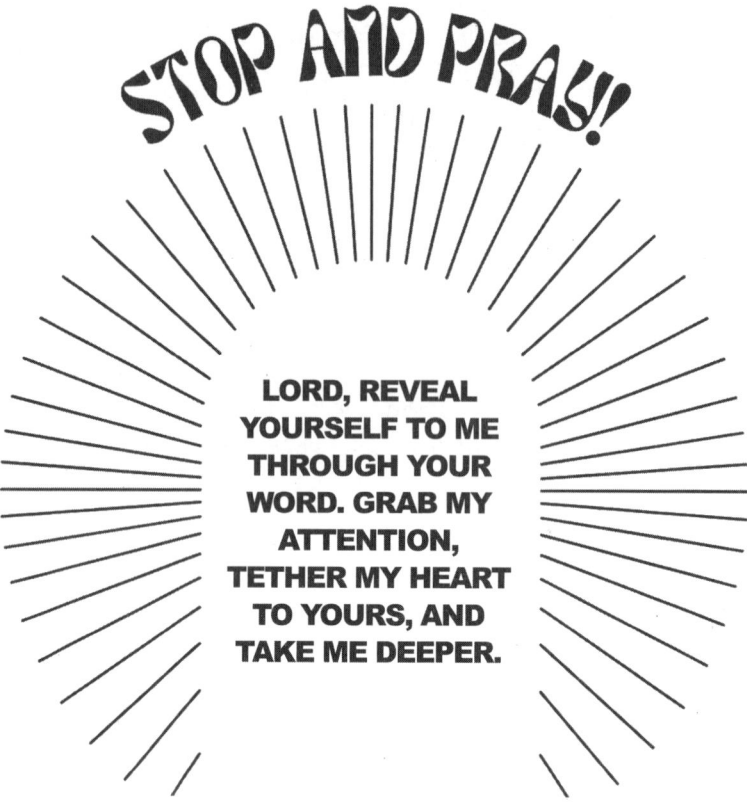

STOP AND PRAY!

LORD, REVEAL YOURSELF TO ME THROUGH YOUR WORD. GRAB MY ATTENTION, TETHER MY HEART TO YOURS, AND TAKE ME DEEPER.

OK, let's get real. If you read that first line of Matthew and you were confused as to how that was the best attention-grabbing intro the Biblical author could come up with, let's dive into the background and context of this particular Gospel to shed some light.

The Gospel of Matthew is the first book in the New Testament. "Gospel" is the term used to describe the four back-to-back books of Matthew, Mark, Luke, and John, which tell the story of Jesus's life and ministry on earth. We call it Matthew's Gospel because its authorship is traditionally attributed to Matthew, one of Jesus's twelve disciples. Pre-Jesus, Matthew was a tax collector, pretty much a traitor to His Jewish heritage, and a guy who was easy to hate. But Jesus called Him straight from his tax booth to boots-on-the-ground ministry, radically transforming his life and capturing

01 / BEAUTIFUL KINGDOM

so much of his heart that Matthew wrote a beautiful account of the things He witnessed as He walked with Jesus.

Each Gospel has its own flavor. We label Mark as the short and to-the-point Gospel, Luke as the detailed Gospel, and John as the out-of-the-box Gospel. Matthew is known as the "Jewish Gospel." Now, that doesn't mean it's only relevant to Jewish people or that if you're not Jewish, you're excluded from the Matthew club. In fact, Matthew is exceptionally critical of the Jewish leaders in His account! But it does help us get a good framework for which audience he originally had in mind as he was writing. And it explains why his Gospel contains over 130 Old Testament callbacks, moments that any good Jew would be able to immediately recall. Here's the simplest way to say it:

Matthew is the only gospel written by a Jew to the Jews about their Jewish Messiah, the King of the Jews.[1]

That lens helps us understand why the first line is actually *super* attention grabbing for the original audience.

> **"THIS IS THE GENEALOGY OF JESUS THE MESSIAH THE SON OF DAVID, THE SON OF ABRAHAM:"**
> Matthew 1:1

Matthew kicks things off with a bold statement. He's proclaiming that Jesus is the promised Messiah, the One prophesied all throughout the Old Testament to be the coming Savior. The One who would rescue a war-torn and oppressed people. Any ancient Jew would read those words and be electrified. It was dangerous, life-altering, and radical.

Jesus, the Messiah.

Armed with that context, let's jump into our study of Matthew and see what God wants to show us, teach us, and reveal to us through His Word. But here's a little disclaimer: *We can't hit everything*. Even John (another Gospel author) wrote that, "If every one of [the things Jesus did] were written down . . . the whole world would not have room for the books that would be written" (John 21:25). If the Biblical authors couldn't cover everything, we certainly can't! So let's take this journey through Matthew at our own pace, diving into specific moments as they come and asking the Lord for extra guidance on parts we could never do justice in a ten-week study.

In fact, to help us zoom in and narrow our focus for this study, let's find out what Matthew's main message was as He was writing. We won't have to search too hard though, because His "thesis statement" is actually repeated *thirty-three times* in his gospel. I won't make you guess! In fact, let's use it as our first point:

1. JESUS CAME TO ANNOUNCE THE KINGDOM OF HEAVEN.

I spent months researching the book of Matthew in preparation for this study. It was such a special time because it felt like I just got to hang out with Jesus. I got to know the tone of His voice, got more familiar with His likes and dislikes, and found myself referring to Him in casual conversation like I would a close friend. (My heart is that you would feel the same way at the end of this ten-week journey!) During that research, I noticed that almost every single theologian who had studied Matthew for any period of time would say the same thing: Matthew saw Jesus's message during His ministry as proclaiming the Kingdom of Heaven. Literally, every book I read pointed back to that one phrase! So we can pretty safely say it's Matthew's thesis statement. I'm not one to try to reinvent the wheel, so we'll use

01 / BEAUTIFUL KINGDOM

the proclamation of the Kingdom of Heaven as our guiding message, too.

The first time we see that crucial phrase is in Matthew 3. Let's check it out!

Read Matthew 3:1–12.

+ FILL IN THE BLANKS FROM MATTHEW 3:1–2.

"IN THOSE DAYS _____ THE _____ CAME, PREACHING IN THE WILDERNESS OF JUDEA AND SAYING, 'REPENT, FOR THE _____ ____ _____ HAS COME NEAR.'"

OK, OK . . . I can guess what might be going on in your head right now.

Who is John the Baptist?

How is it Jesus's message if John's the one who says it?

Why are we in the wilderness? What about baby Jesus in the manger?

Yeah, we had to skip some really important stuff. But don't panic! When you have the chance, feel free to spend some time looking over chapters 1 and 2 to catch yourself up to speed and remind yourself of Jesus's early years. But honestly, John the Baptist's appearance in this Gospel is just as abrupt and seemingly random as you think. It's crucial to remember that Matthew was writing for an ancient Jewish audience. For them, the scriptural hyperlink he offers in verse 3 is more than enough to clue them in on John's role in the story.

BEAUTIFUL KINGDOM

Matthew quickly and succinctly labels John as the herald for the Messiah, the one crying out *literally in the wilderness* that the King is coming soon. He's like the flower girl at a wedding who prepares the way for the bride. John's role was to ensure the children of Israel's hearts were ready for the main event: Jesus. He's dropping truth-bombs like flower petals, creating a beautiful runway on which Jesus will enter the scene.

So it makes sense that John's message is the same as Jesus's! He's paving the way, ferociously preparing the hearts of God's people for the shock wave he knows is coming through the Messiah. He's asking them to "repent," or turn away from their sins, and baptizing them, eager for Jesus to come on the scene and be greeted with hearts that are ready to join His mission.

> **TAKE IT DEEPER...**
> You can find John the Baptist's origin story in Luke 1:5–25. His birth was super miraculous, and it's obvious that God had set him apart for big things even before he was born. Read through it and see what stands out to you!

Before we go any further, we gotta be sure we know what we're talking about. What is the Kingdom of Heaven? Here's a nerdy definition I found:

Kingdom of heaven: Synonymous with "kingdom of God." Both expressions refer to the time when God's rule would be enacted on earth as it is in heaven. Biblical writers often used "heaven" as a way of referring to God and His abode without having to use the divine name (Yahweh).[2]

Basically, the Kingdom of Heaven is a name for what it will look like when God reenters the scene and redeems a broken world. For the ancient Jews, constantly oppressed by foreign governments, this was more than just a metaphysical ideal. It was a political reality they were holding out for! For them, the coming of the Messiah would mean a literal *kingdom* where God ruled here on Earth. The Messiah was expected to overthrow the Roman government, wage

01 / BEAUTIFUL KINGDOM

a bloody war, and restore Israel to its monarchy like it was in the time of King David.

Now, we don't want to give away any spoilers, but . . . it doesn't quite turn out that way. In fact, the rest of the book of Matthew will be filled with the tension between what the Jews *expected* the coming Kingdom to be like and what Jesus was actually bringing to fruition. Even John the Baptist was thrown off when Jesus came on the scene, which we can read as we continue on in the Scripture.

Read Matthew 3:13–15.

And there He is! Fully grown, thirty-year-old Jesus has stepped on the scene! This is *the* moment, the arrival John has spent his whole life preparing for. He should bow down in worship, start crying hysterically, and beg Jesus to tell Him all His plans for a new regime. But that's not what happens. This is so crazy to read, but the Bible says that in John's first documented interaction with an on-mission Jesus, John *disagreed with Him*.

What!?

Guys, this is wild! Scripture never ceases to amaze me because it's just so real. Honestly, I think most of us would have responded in the exact same way. I mean, put yourself in John's shoes! He prepped his whole life to usher in the Messiah (his cousin, Jesus!) and he probably lay awake at night dreaming about how He'd make His big entrance, perhaps storming onto the scene with a sword in one hand and the Torah in the other. He'd come and take control, leading with zeal and cleansing the world of the nasty influences bombarding the Jewish people on all sides.

But instead, Jesus walked up to John, got into the river with him, and asked to be baptized. Really, John's confusion is understandable!

> **"BUT JOHN TRIED TO DETER HIM, SAYING, 'I NEED TO BE BAPTIZED BY YOU, AND DO YOU COME TO ME?'"**
> Matthew 3:14

This misunderstanding brings us to our next point.

2. EXPECT THE UNEXPECTED.

Have you ever heard the saying, "Don't meet your heroes"? We have this human tendency to paint an image in our minds of people we observe from a distance and create this whole persona for them up in our heads. Like, in my mind, Taylor Swift and I are close friends and we would immediately bond and have hours of things to chat about if we ran into each other on the street. But I'm guessing if I really met her, she'd be different than how I imagined.

Often, we do the same thing with Jesus. We listen to pastors, friends, and podcasts talk about Him, and we paint this incomplete picture of Him in our head. We assume we know how He'd react in certain situations, we confidently decide when we think He will act and who He'll go to battle for. But then, we meet Him. We spend real, personal time with Him through His Word. We begin to listen for His voice and His whispers through the Spirit. There, in that blossoming friendship and intimacy, we find ourselves surprised.

He says things we don't expect Him to say. He does things we don't expect Him to do. We find that He's better than we imagined. Better, but different.

John the Baptist was expecting a conquering king, and what did he get? A humble cousin, willing to bend low and get on his level. You see it, right? *Better, but different.*

01 / BEAUTIFUL KINGDOM

+ CAN YOU THINK OF A TIME WHEN JESUS SURPRISED YOU? WHEN HE MOVED IN A WAY YOU DIDN'T EXPECT? WRITE YOUR EXPERIENCE DOWN IN THE SPACE BELOW.

I love Jesus's response to John's pushback.

> **"JESUS REPLIED, 'LET IT BE SO NOW; IT IS PROPER FOR US TO DO THIS TO FULFILL ALL RIGHTEOUSNESS.' THEN JOHN CONSENTED."**
> **Matthew 3:15**

He didn't turn around and find someone else because of John's surprise. He didn't even rebuke John for trying to correct Him! Instead, we can picture Jesus looking John in the eyes and letting him in on the secrets of His Kingdom.

You see, Jesus didn't *need* to be baptized. He had no sin to repent for. He didn't *need* to let John, a sinful man, dunk Him in the water. But He chose to do it. Why? Because He wanted to identify with us. Jesus's baptism, the symbolic start to His ministry, set the tone for the rest of His life on earth. Jesus was a Messiah who was willing to get on our level. He was willing to go low, to get dirty. He knew His people were in desperate need of cleansing of sin, in desperate need to get in the Jordan River and start fresh. So He started there, too. That's the secret He let John in on! Jesus Christ desired to humble Himself. He desired to understand what His people were going through.

He desired to identify with the very sinners He would die for.

Wow! We're only a few verses in and I already feel like crying. I love this Jesus! Do you feel yourself getting a little closer to Him? Getting a little more familiar with His character? Sister, let me tell you. This is just the beginning.

Let's go ahead and wrap up our Scripture reading for this week with what is, in my opinion, one of the coolest moments in the whole Bible.

Read Matthew 3:16–17.

We could write ten books on these two verses alone. We could explore the symbolism of Jesus emerging from the Jordan River just like the ancient Israelites, the magnitude of the Heavens opening over Him, the significance of the presence of the three persons of the Trinity active together in one moment, the deep meaning of the Holy Spirit's appearance like a dove . . . The list goes on! But for the sake of this chapter of this study at this time, I want to focus on what God said as He spoke over His son, Jesus.

+ FILL IN THE BLANKS FROM MATTHEW 3:17.

"AND A VOICE FROM HEAVEN SAID, 'THIS IS MY SON, WHOM I _____; WITH HIM I AM WELL PLEASED.'"

01 / BEAUTIFUL KINGDOM

God, Creator of the Universe, King of the Heavens, Father of the Messiah, spoke audibly. He addressed His people, the ones who had long since abandoned Him, the ones for whom He was about to sacrifice His only son. He spoke, knowing they could all hear Him. And what was His message?

Love.

3. GOD'S STARTING POINT IS ALWAYS LOVE.

We could sit here all day just letting that fact sink in. God had one moment to speak, a moment He could have used to admonish, punish, condemn, call for change, stir to action, declare His power ... And He chose to speak of His *love*. Talk about unexpected! But that's just the thing. In the midst of the unexpected, *we can always expect God's love.*

All the way back in Exodus, God came down to speak to Moses in a cloud, and how did He choose to describe Himself?

> "THE LORD, THE LORD, THE COMPASSIONATE AND GRACIOUS GOD, SLOW TO ANGER, ABOUNDING IN <u>LOVE</u> AND FAITHFULNESS, MAINTAINING <u>LOVE</u> TO THOUSANDS, AND FORGIVING WICKEDNESS, REBELLION AND SIN."
> Exodus 34:6–7a, emphasis added

We are about to embark on a journey that may be tough. Reading God's Word, especially the true story of Jesus's life and ministry, His death and resurrection, has a tendency to challenge you. It has

BEAUTIFUL KINGDOM

a tendency to upend long-held beliefs, to make you dig deeper and think harder than you have before. Just like the early Christians had the wrong idea of the Kingdom, we often find ourselves misled and in need of redirection.

But we're not doing all that exposed and unprotected! No, we're jumping in completely covered by the abounding *love* of our God. Jesus knew this secret, one spoken over Him as He began the hardest mission any person would ever have to endure. He knew He could rely on the Father's love.

Can you?

+ BE HONEST . . . HOW HAVE YOU BEEN VIEWING GOD THESE DAYS? DO YOU SEE HIM AS LOVING? HARSH? DISTANT? KIND? PROCESS YOUR FEELINGS BELOW.

01 / BEAUTIFUL KINGDOM

+ IT'S CRUCIAL THAT WE START THIS STUDY OFF ON A SOLID FOUNDATION OF GOD'S LOVE FOR US. TAKE A MOMENT AND ASK GOD TO SHOW HIS LOVE TO YOU IN A NEW WAY. WHAT DO YOU FEEL HIM SHOWING YOU? JOT DOWN YOUR STREAM OF CONSCIOUSNESS IN THE SPACE BELOW.

I came across a quote the other day that really hit me, especially as I read this moment in Scripture.

Repent of your small thoughts of God's heart. Repent and let him love you.[3]

BEAUTIFUL KINGDOM

Jesus came to usher in the Kingdom of Heaven, a kingdom that's upside-down, a kingdom that smashes expectations, crushes barriers, and shocks us all. Yes, it's unexpected and, at times, uncomfortable. But it is deeply rooted and reliably founded on the *love* of God. The whole Bible is a love story between God and His people! Every act, work, miracle, and mission is a picture painted of God's great love for us, His treasured children.

I beg you, don't try to understand the Bible without first knowing how loved you are by the One who wrote it. Sure, Jesus is about to tell us the right way to live, He's going to teach us and challenge us. He's going to guide us through these confusing, wild, and stretching years of college with wisdom and authority. But all of that is an overflow and outpouring of the love of God. Just like God did as He commissioned His Son at that river, *start with love*.

Here's what I want to leave you with, a subset of the mission of this whole study of Matthew. Jesus announced the Kingdom of Heaven. And it's beautiful.

My mission in this study is to get you to open your eyes and your heart to gaze upon the wonder and the beauty of Jesus. To see the obviously shiny parts of His message *and* the tough, hard to understand parts of His message as beautiful. It's not just a long-awaited Kingdom, not just a shocking Kingdom, not just a needed Kingdom . . . It's a beautiful Kingdom.

> "ONE THING I ASK FROM THE LORD, THIS ONLY DO I SEEK: THAT I MAY DWELL IN THE HOUSE OF THE LORD ALL THE DAYS OF MY LIFE, TO GAZE ON THE BEAUTY OF THE LORD AND TO SEEK HIM IN HIS TEMPLE."
> **Psalm 27:4**

01 / BEAUTIFUL KINGDOM

Let's start there, where God started. Deeply rooted in His radical love, we can gaze on the beauty of the Lord in His temple. We can watch Jesus's life and ministry with Heaven's eyes. Isn't He radiant?

BEAUTIFUL KINGDOM

CONVERSATION STARTERS

1. Be honest... How are you feeling about God's Word these days? Distant? Hungry? Bored? All in?

2. John the Baptist was shocked by the way Jesus chose to move. Think back on a time when God moved in a way that was different than how you were expecting. How did you respond?

01 / **BEAUTIFUL KINGDOM**

3. God's starting point is always love. Where do you think you're starting as you begin this study? What's the condition of your heart? Where's your faith at in this season?

4. Let's vision cast! Spend some time in prayer, asking God to show you what He wants to teach you through this study. Where do you hope to be by the end of these ten weeks?

HOW TO PRAY

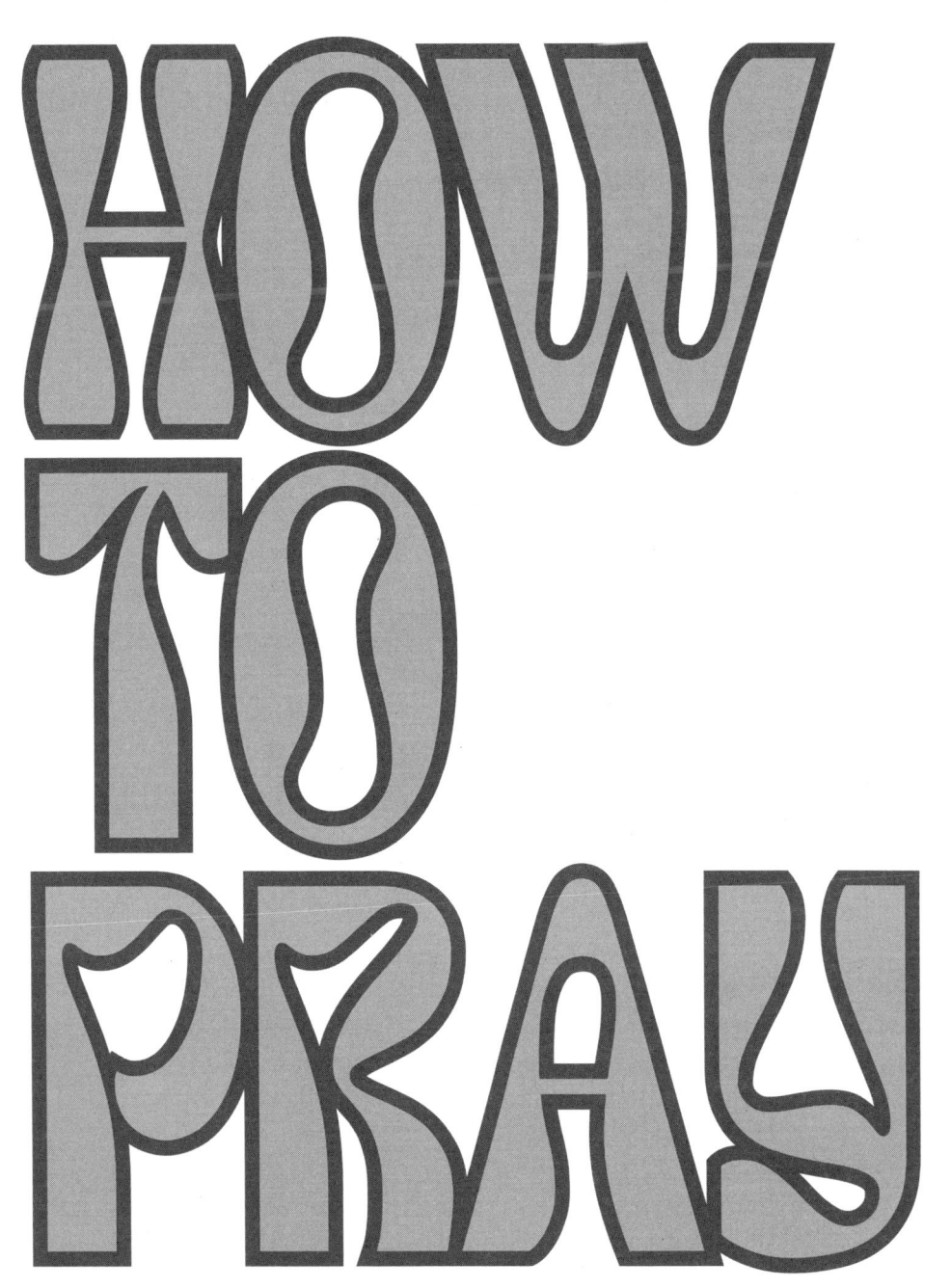

CHAPTER 2

BEAUTIFUL KINGDOM

HOW TO PRAY

Matthew 6:5 - 13

When was the first time you prayed? I mean, *really* prayed. Can you remember?

Maybe it was a soft whisper in your room before you went to bed when you were too young to understand what you were doing. Maybe it was at church, praying along with the pastor. Maybe it was at a high school worship night—the moment when the Lord caught your attention for the first time. Or maybe it was in a moment of panic when you felt like you had nowhere else to turn.

Prayer can either feel so normal or so alien; either a typical part of our lives or some practice only hyper-spiritual people can do. It can get . . . complicated.

So we're going to reset; reconnect to that first time it felt real and necessary. Prayer is a *gift* from God! A supernatural and intimate

02 / HOW TO PRAY

way we get to connect with our Heavenly Father. We don't need to overcomplicate it, hyper-spiritualize it, or run away from it kicking and screaming.

This week, let's learn how to pray. But I'm not just going to make up some best practices, create some new life-rhythms, or tell you what I think about prayer. No, we have the blessing of a teaching straight from the mouth of our Savior! Jesus, in His ministry here on earth, took the time to teach us how to pray. What a joy it is to know that we don't have to try to figure it out on our own! Praise God!

And the crazy thing is, the reason He taught us how to pray is because *somebody asked*.

+ FILL IN THE BLANKS FROM LUKE 11:1.

"ONE DAY JESUS WAS PRAYING IN A CERTAIN PLACE. WHEN HE FINISHED, ONE OF HIS DISCIPLES SAID TO HIM, 'LORD, _____ ____ TO _____, JUST AS JOHN TAUGHT HIS DISCIPLES.'"

This is so wild to think about! All these years later, we have the *gift* of a teaching on prayer straight from Jesus's mouth because one of His disciples was bold enough to ask. That's my challenge for you this week! Would you be bold enough to ask God to take you deeper? To share His secrets with you? I know we all come into this conversation around prayer with different fears, doubts, and hurts. Whether you've never prayed out loud, you don't think your prayers really matter, or you've never thought to pray at all, I believe that God wants to reveal something new to you as you read His Word! So let's open up this holy and sacred gift and allow the Lord to move.

It's going to be beautiful!

STOP AND PRAY!

LORD, THANK YOU FOR THE GIFT OF YOUR WORD. WOULD YOU CONTINUE TO TEACH ME HOW TO PRAY? PLEASE OPEN UP MY HEART AND DRAW ME CLOSER TO YOU.

For this chapter, we're going to focus on ten verses from Matthew chapter 6. And I know, I know... We skipped ahead! There is so much good stuff we missed in chapters 4 and 5, so I highly encourage you to go and read them on your own time. Between where we left off last week and where we pick up this week, Jesus was tested in the wilderness by the devil, began announcing the Kingdom, called Simon Peter and James to be His disciples, performed miracles, and sat down to deliver the most famous speech ever given: the Sermon on the Mount.

Now, some things to note about the Sermon on the Mount to give us context as we dive into this teaching... You can view this message as a proclamation of sorts. It's Jesus painting this image of the coming Kingdom (you know, the one we talked about last week!) and inviting His listeners to take a peek behind the curtain

02 / HOW TO PRAY

and see the beauty Jesus came to bring. The common thread throughout is Jesus's attention to the heart and the motives behind our actions. He's throwing off the chains of empty, formulaic religion and calling us into true purity of heart and union with God like it was all the way back in the garden of Eden.

It's in the middle of that famous sermon where we begin our reading this week. After delivering shocking, convicting, and life-changing teachings (again, please go read these chapters—you won't regret it!), Jesus begins to talk about prayer, prompted, as we learned from Luke's Gospel, by a simple question.

Read Matthew 6:5–8.

I love how He starts this off! Jesus isn't messing around!

+ COPY DOWN THE FIRST FOUR WORDS OF MATTHEW 6:5.

And when you pray . . . Notice He doesn't say, "If you pray" or, "In case you want to pray" or, "On the off chance that you pray." No way! For Jesus, the fact that we will be praying is a given. Maybe He knew that a bunch of college women would be reading His words two thousand years later and He wanted to give us a good starting point. Prayer is important! We are called to do it; it's a non-negotiable for followers of Jesus. So if you've been wondering if you really need to, let these words from Jesus be your wake-up call! We gotta pray.

Think of this as God's invitation into deeper intimacy with Him. That's what prayer does! It's a tether connecting your heart to your Father's. And Jesus doesn't just tell us to do it because He wants to give us another thing to check off our to-do lists. He calls us deeper into prayer because He loves us. You are on the edge of something wonderful and exciting that God is inviting you into through the gift of prayer.

And what does He say next? Continuing on with the flow of the rest of His sermon, Jesus addresses the *heart* of prayer.

1. IN SECRET

I never really spent consistent time with the Lord in prayer and in the Word until my freshman year of college. I remember waking up early in my dorm—while my roommate was still asleep—and sitting at my little university-issued desk and turning my teal blue lamp on. Every morning, I'd sit at that desk with my Bible open and a bowl of Froot Loops in front of me and talk to the Lord.

Can you relate? Have you spent those moments with the Lord that feel so intimate just between you and Him? OK, maybe it wasn't a dorm room but beside a campfire at night. On the floor of your childhood bedroom. In the back of a church auditorium during a worship night . . . Whatever the setting, do you know what it feels like to watch the Lord create something unique in the secret, hidden moments?

Those tender, quiet meetings with God, over time, build something special inside of us. It reminds me of what Jesus describes in these verses.

> **"BUT WHEN YOU PRAY, GO INTO YOUR ROOM, CLOSE THE DOOR AND PRAY TO YOUR FATHER,"**
> **Matthew 6:6a**

But why does He tell us to do that? Does prayer only work when done alone, in a private room? Certainly not, right?

I think Jesus describes this secret space to remind us of the motive behind why we pray. He reminds us that we shouldn't pray just to be seen (though I have been guilty of that time and

02 / HOW TO PRAY

time again) and that we shouldn't try to find a magic spell to say that will make Him actually answer our prayers. Prayer, at its core, should originate from the secret, unseen place of our heart. We pray *for*, *to*, and *because of* God. It's union with Him, an unseen relationship we build with daily repetition.

> **"THEN YOUR FATHER, WHO SEES WHAT IS DONE IN SECRET, WILL REWARD YOU."**
> **Matthew 6:6b**

So even before we learn how to pray, we need to evaluate *why* we pray. Do you pray for attention? Do you pray to look like a good Christian? Do you pray because you're worried that if you don't bad things will happen? Do you pray just to get your requests answered?

Or, do you pray because you want to seek the Lord while He may be found (Isaiah 55:6)? Do you pray because He promises the personal, intimate reward of His presence (Matthew 6:6)? Do you pray because you're desperate for it (Psalm 42:1)?

+ WHAT IS YOUR CURRENT ATTITUDE TOWARD PRAYER? WHAT MIGHT YOUR MOTIVATIONS BE? (USE THE EXAMPLES LISTED ABOVE AS A STARTING POINT TO THINK THROUGH YOUR ANSWER. ARE THERE ANY THAT YOU RELATE TO?)

BEAUTIFUL KINGDOM

The cool thing is, Jesus doesn't just stop at telling us to value secret prayer. He actually models it for us time and time again in the Gospels! He is often found going off to a mountainside to pray, taking a walk on the beach to talk to His Father, and disappearing to commune with God in secret. Y'all, if Jesus needed unseen time in prayer, how much more do we!?

Start in the secret place. Hold God to His Word! See if secret prayers, time spent where no one can see, really do make an impact. Watch as He softens your heart, as He refines and remakes you in that dorm room, on the floor of your childhood bedroom, or at the kitchen table in the early hours of the morning.

Now, we could probably spend hours on just those four verses, but for the sake of time, we have to keep moving. Go ahead and read Matthew 6:9–13.

> **TAKE IT DEEPER...**
> If you want to learn more about praying in secret and the value of an unseen relationship with the Lord, I recommend checking out *Unseen* by Sara Hagerty and *Secrets of the Secret Place* by Bob Sorge.

"THIS, THEN, IS HOW YOU SHOULD PRAY:"
Matthew 6:9

Here, after explaining the heart behind prayer, Jesus jumps right into a clear, repeatable teaching on *how* to pray. So clear and repeatable, in fact, that it's probably the most famous prayer ever, recited at bedtimes and in church services around the world for thousands of years. We call it "the Lord's Prayer."

2. HOW TO PRAY

Before we go any further, I want you to try it out. Wherever you are, take a minute or two to read the whole prayer out loud, just

02 / HOW TO PRAY

as so many generations of Christians have done since the time of Jesus.

> *OUR FATHER IN HEAVEN,*
> *HALLOWED BE YOUR NAME,*
> *YOUR KINGDOM COME,*
> *YOUR WILL BE DONE,*
> *ON EARTH AS IT IS IN HEAVEN.*
> *GIVE US THIS DAY OUR DAILY BREAD.*
> *AND FORGIVE US OUR DEBTS,*
> *AS WE ALSO HAVE FORGIVEN OUR DEBTORS.*
> *AND LEAD US NOT INTO TEMPTATION,*
> *BUT DELIVER US FROM THE EVIL ONE.*

+ DOES ANY PART STAND OUT TO YOU? HOW DID IT FEEL TO PRAY IT OUT LOUD?

Whether you grew up praying this or you've just heard it for the first time now, we all can admit . . . It's pretty awesome. We've already established that it's a gift to have a teaching on prayer from Jesus, but how much more so is it to have an example of how to pray! We get to learn straight from Him, to literally say what He said. This is wild!

BEAUTIFUL KINGDOM

Now, there are a million different ways we could break down this prayer and learn from it, and many, many scholars have gone before me in squeezing this lemon for all it's worth. For our purposes this week, we're going to keep it simple. Think of this like an introductory lesson to prayer, a tiny toe-dip into the ocean of wisdom God offers us on the subject. So if you're left wanting more... Perfect! Dig deeper! Dive in!

We can split Jesus's prayer into two parts: verses 9–10 and verses 11–13. We'll call them "honor" and "dependence." Let's dive into honor first!

+ COPY DOWN THE FIRST TWO VERSES OF THE LORD'S PRAYER IN THE SPACE BELOW.

Picture this: You're in that secret place, maybe your dorm room before your eight a.m. class, and you sit down, ready to pray. Where do you start?

According to Jesus, we start with *honor*. He tells the Father that His name is "hallowed" (the Passion Translation says it like this: *May the glory of your name be the center on which our lives turn*). Then He calls on the Kingdom, which is exactly what we'd expect as expert Matthew readers! He asks God to be in control, giving the Father the power, the honor, and all the glory.

What might that look like for us? You are definitely welcome to pray Jesus's exact words (you can't ever go wrong doing that!), but what about when you want to free-form it? It could look like beginning with gratitude for what God's done in your

02 / HOW TO PRAY

life, affirming His goodness and reminding yourself of it, or resurrendering your heart with words like, "I give you my heart" or, "I trust that you are in control."

Here's the bottom line: Effective and powerful prayer begins with an all-consuming desire to see our God honored and respected as the holy God He is.[1] That's where we need to start! Next, Jesus shows us where to go from there.

+ COPY DOWN THE LAST THREE VERSES OF THE LORD'S PRAYER.

The other basic component of prayer is *dependence*. It's clear that Jesus wanted His disciples, and us by extension, to live in a state of constant dependence on God's provision.[2] He prayed for daily bread, forgiveness, protection, and help. I love this step because it's so simple! We often find ourselves getting caught up in the pressures of performance, constantly trying to be the best Christian and beating ourselves up with shame and condemnation when we fall short. Jesus sees it differently. He says to go to our Father. *He* will provide everything we need to be who He is calling us to be.

So many of us fall into the trap of independence, even in our prayer lives. We list out the things we've done wrong (which is a great practice! God definitely wants us to confess our sins to Him!), then we just tell Him we'll try to do better. What if instead, we confess our shortcomings to God and ask for a new revelation of His forgiveness? A new revelation of His power? In dependence on Him, you are allowing God to work through you. Trust me, He can do it a lot better than you can.

+ WHICH PART OF PRAYER (HONOR OR DEPENDENCE) DO YOU WANT TO GROW IN? WHY?

OK. Let's get real. Did you just read all that teaching on prayer and still feel... Unequipped? Uninterested? Confused? Overwhelmed? I totally get it! You are *so* not alone in feeling that way. Since prayer is so key and crucial to our relationships with God, the enemy loves to attack us there. He loves to get in our heads and try to dissuade us from running to the Father in prayer. So we're going to take some time to address the elephant in the room. Sure, you know how to pray... but what's getting in the way?

3. YOU CAN PRAY.

Think back to the beginning of this chapter. What started this whole conversation on prayer in the first place?

> "ONE DAY JESUS WAS PRAYING IN A CERTAIN PLACE. WHEN HE FINISHED, ONE OF HIS DISCIPLES SAID TO HIM, 'LORD, TEACH US TO PRAY,"
> Luke 11:1a-b

02 / HOW TO PRAY

Even Jesus's disciples, the guys who walked with Him intimately and consistently, were a little confused and wary about prayer. It's alright that we are, too! But just as Jesus answered them then, He will also answer us now.

When I was in college, I went through a phase where I was wondering whether my prayers really mattered. *God is sovereign,* I'd say. *He's gonna do what He's gonna do. Why would it matter what I pray?* Please tell me I wasn't alone in that confusion! Also in college, I had a friend who found herself getting nervous any time she had to pray out loud. No matter how many girls we sent her way in need of prayer, she'd get clammy and try to find an escape route. Sound like you? I've met women who don't pray at all and women who pray all day long but are frustrated because their prayers don't get answered. It's an issue so many of us relate to: prayer can be hard.

THINK IT THROUGH!

+ WHAT HOLDS YOU BACK THE MOST WHEN IT COMES TO PRAYER?

BEAUTIFUL KINGDOM

+ BE HONEST . . . WHAT'S YOUR PRAYER LIFE LIKE THESE DAYS? WHAT DO YOU WANT IT TO BE LIKE?

Whatever your holdup is, I want to encourage you. *You can pray.* God created you to pray! He's given you all the tools! He's given you His Spirit to nudge your heart to the Father! And He's given you His Word when doubts, fears, and misdirections start to creep in.

For the girl who feels like her prayers don't matter, God says . . .

> "ASK AND IT WILL BE GIVEN TO YOU; SEEK AND YOU WILL FIND; KNOCK AND THE DOOR WILL BE OPENED TO YOU. FOR EVERYONE WHO ASKS RECEIVES; THE ONE WHO SEEKS FINDS; AND TO THE ONE WHO KNOCKS, THE DOOR WILL BE OPENED."
> **Matthew 7:7-8**

For the girl who's intimidated to pray out loud, God says . . .

> "I HAVE PUT MY WORDS IN YOUR MOUTH AND COVERED YOU WITH THE SHADOW OF MY HAND—"
> **Isaiah 51:16a**

02 / HOW TO PRAY

For the girl who is scared to pray over a friend, God says . . .

> **"THEREFORE CONFESS YOUR SINS TO EACH OTHER AND PRAY FOR EACH OTHER SO THAT YOU MAY BE HEALED. THE PRAYER OF A RIGHTEOUS PERSON IS POWERFUL AND EFFECTIVE."**
> **James 5:16**

And for all of us wondering if we should pray at all, God reminds us . . .

> **"AND PRAY IN THE SPIRIT ON ALL OCCASIONS WITH ALL KINDS OF PRAYERS AND REQUESTS. WITH THIS IN MIND, BE ALERT AND ALWAYS KEEP ON PRAYING FOR ALL THE LORD'S PEOPLE."**
> **Ephesians 6:18**

I mean, I'm feeling hyped up already! *You can pray!* When you feel like you're in over your head, run to the Word. And remember:

Prayer isn't about us. It's all about God.

We are so blessed to have this wonderful opportunity to connect our hearts to our Father's heart. What a gift! So today, dip your toe in. Allow God to take you a little bit deeper, to draw you a little bit closer. He's got your back! Start in the secret place with a tender heart, give Him the honor He deserves, and watch your life change.

CONVERSATION STARTERS

1. Time to get real... How does this whole "prayer" conversation make you feel (nervous, frustrated, excited, convicted, etc.)?

2. How does the way you pray differ from the way Jesus prays? Is there anything you feel called to change about the way you pray?

02 / **HOW TO PRAY**

3. In point three, we found pieces of Scripture that spoke to some of our fears and reservations when it comes to prayer. Which Scripture resonated the most with you? Why?

4. Let's put it into practice! We want to invite your Delight chapter to spend some time in prayer. Start off by getting alone and having an intimate conversation between you and God, using the Lord's Prayer as your guide. Then, group up and pray over each other. What a fun way to activate what we learned!

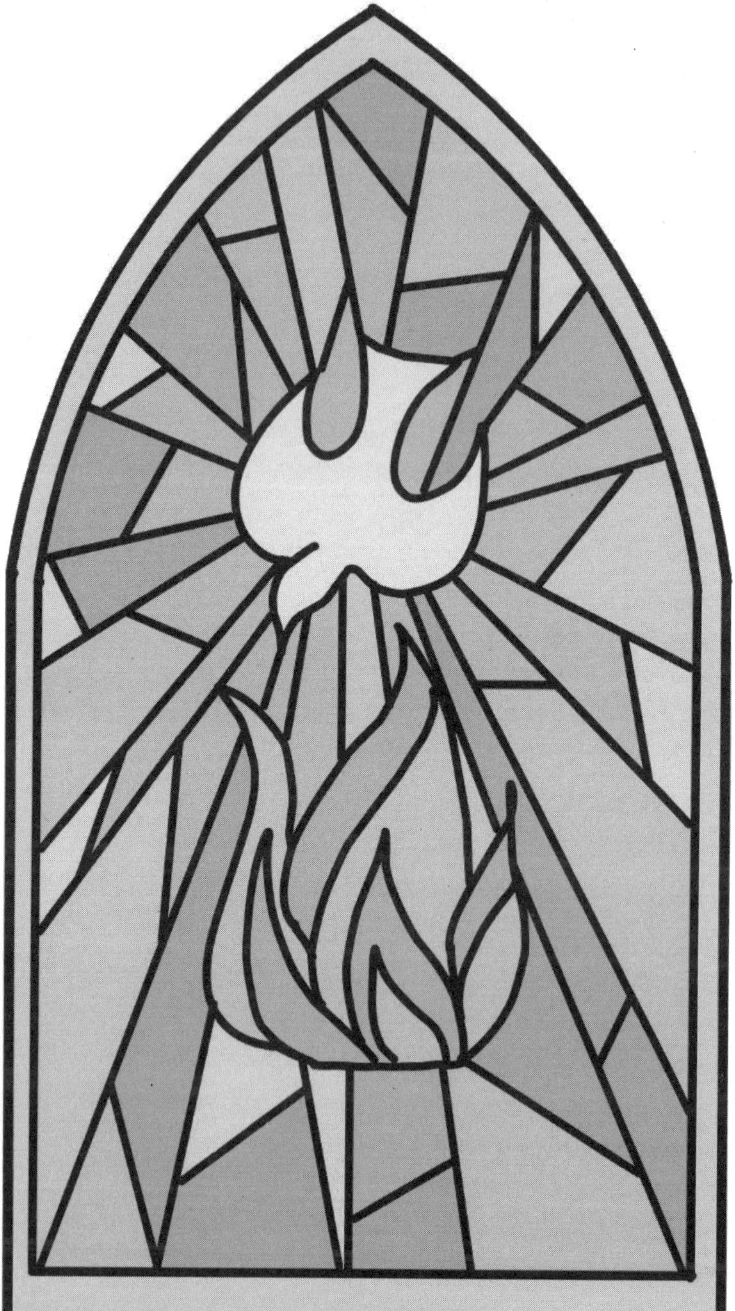

FIRST THINGS FIRST

CHAPTER 3

BEAUTIFUL KINGDOM

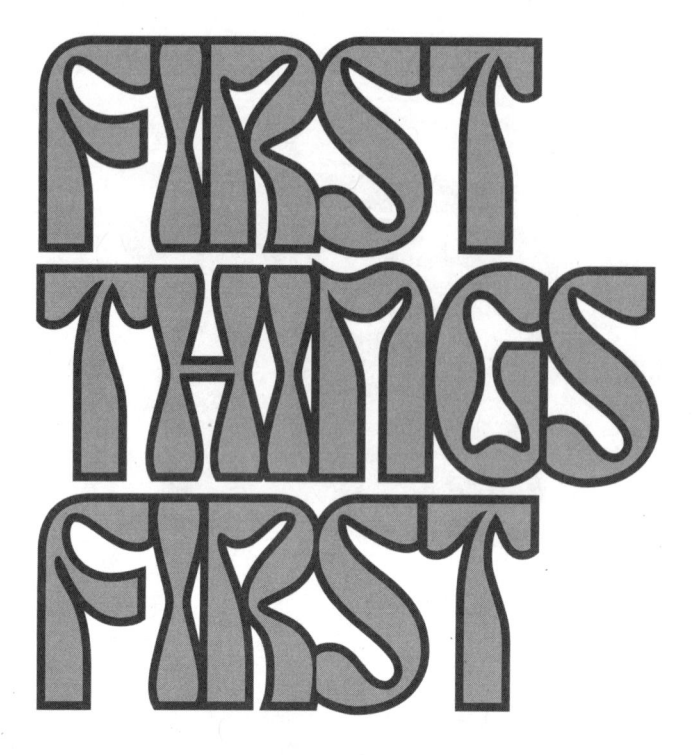

FIRST THINGS FIRST

Matthew 6:25 – 34

What's the biggest struggle in my life? Thank you for asking! It's picking out an outfit.

I think most of us girls can relate. Imagine! You have somewhere to be, your hair's done, your makeup's done, you only have an hour until you need to leave . . .

But you have nothing to wear. *Cue the horror movie screams.*

OK, sure, I'm being a little dramatic. It's not the *biggest* struggle of my life. But it does cause me so much stress! I just want to feel cute, trendy, and on par for the occasion. But I usually end up trying on every single item in my closet, hating it all, crying for a couple minutes, then just throwing on the same outfit I wore the day before and leaving in a grumpy rage.

03 / FIRST THINGS FIRST

I mean, it's a universal struggle, right? The Sunday before-church outfit panic, the first day of class frenzy, that weird time between summer and fall when you have no clue what to wear . . . I'm getting a little panicked just thinking about it! You can laugh all you want if you can't relate, but picking out an outfit can be fairly traumatic. (If you're wondering where I'm going with this, hang in there.)

Did you know that Jesus addressed that struggle in the Sermon on the Mount? You don't believe me? Read the Scripture!

Read Matthew 6:25–34.

Wow, we really do have a high priest who can empathize with our weaknesses (Hebrews 4:15). He knows the struggle.

> **"DO NOT WORRY ABOUT . . . WHAT YOU WILL WEAR."**
> **Matthew 6:25**

That's a word from the Lord! We can close our books and go home!

But, actually . . . I don't think that's all Jesus is trying to say here. Sure, He doesn't want us to stress about our outfits. But when I read this Scripture, I think there's a much deeper—and honestly much more important—meaning.

Jesus doesn't want us to worry *at all*. About anything. Sound impossible? I know. But let's dive in and see what He has for us.

STOP AND PRAY!

GOD, THANK YOU FOR THE COUNTLESS OPPORTUNITIES FOR JOY THAT YOUR WORD BRINGS. THANK YOU FOR CARING ABOUT THE LITTLE THINGS IN MY LIFE AND THE BIG THINGS. TEACH ME SOMETHING NEW THIS WEEK AND DRAW ME CLOSER.

This week we're going to talk about worry, and that can bring up lots of different reactions. Maybe you've been going to church your whole life and you're getting a little sick of reading this Scripture over and over again. Maybe you struggle with clinical anxiety and you hate it when people tell you to just pray it away. Maybe you worry all the time and you're desperate for a solution from the Lord so you can finally have some peace. I want you to know, I acknowledge all those feelings! God can meet you right where you are. But whether you've read this passage a million times or you've never seen it before, I believe there's something God wants to show you. We just need to be willing to receive.

So let's take this Scripture bit by bit with open hands. Here's where we'll start:

03 / FIRST THINGS FIRST

+ FILL IN THE BLANKS FROM MATTHEW 6:25.

"THEREFORE I TELL YOU, _____ _____ _____ ABOUT YOUR LIFE, WHAT YOU WILL EAT OR DRINK; OR ABOUT YOUR BODY, WHAT YOU WILL WEAR. IS NOT LIFE MORE THAN FOOD, AND THE BODY MORE THAN CLOTHES?"

1. JESUS ISN'T WORRIED.

I think it's crucial that we start this conversation with Jesus. So often, we begin with a focus on ourselves; we list all the things we're worried about, try to decide which ones are worth worrying about and which aren't, then we try to pull ourselves up by our bootstraps and act like we aren't worried anymore when we totally are. But that's probably where we've been getting our wires crossed! Starting a conversation about worry with more worry seems . . . counterproductive. Let's start by looking at Jesus: the One who didn't worry.

Between where we stopped last week with the Lord's Prayer and this week's passage, Jesus taught about fasting and what our heart toward money should be. (Again, please go read it on your own time! I promise it's worth it.) This teaching on worry feels like a natural continuation from there; almost like He's countering peoples' concerns before they voice them. *But what would we do without money, Jesus? How would we survive?*

Don't worry, He says.

Now, from anyone else that would be a super frustrating statement. In my life right now, I'm in a huge waiting and preparation season, and every time I bring it up to my friends, they wind up saying something along the lines of, "Don't stress about it." Has anyone ever said that to you? It's not very helpful, right? Obviously I don't *want* to stress about it! Easy for them to say!

But it's different when it comes from Jesus. Because He actually lived it. He's the living proof that "not worrying" is actually an option. Let's flip around in our Bibles to find some evidence.

+ FLIP TO MATTHEW 8 AND READ VERSES 23–27. WHAT WAS JESUS DOING WHILE THE STORM WAS RAGING?

+ NOW, FLIP TO JOHN 2 AND READ VERSES 1–10. WHO SEEMED STRESSED THAT THEY HAD RUN OUT OF WINE? HOW DID JESUS RESPOND?

+ OK, LAST ONE! FLIP TO LUKE 10 AND READ VERSES 38–42. HOW DID JESUS RESPOND TO MARTHA'S STRESS?

We could probably find a million more examples, but here's the gist: Jesus, time and time again, showed Himself to be calm in the

03 / FIRST THINGS FIRST

face of panic—centered when worry was a real option. So when He says not to worry, He backs it up with His life. He consistently showed us with His actions that there *is* a better way.

Today, Jesus sits at the right hand of God, enthroned in Heaven. So how does He respond to our frantic worries now? I can guarantee that we don't stress Him out. He's not up there panicking, wondering how it's all going to work out. Yes, He understands what we're going through and He feels what we feel so deeply and intimately, but He doesn't wonder if it will be OK. Jesus is at peace because He knows Who's really in control. He knows the victory has already been won.

So let that be an invitation to take a deep breath. Jesus, your friend and Savior, lived a perfect, worry-free life. What if He wants the same for you?

2. GOD HAS PROVEN THAT HE WILL TAKE CARE OF US.

Read Matthew 6:26–32.

+ WHAT STANDS OUT TO YOU FROM THESE VERSES?

BEAUTIFUL KINGDOM

I love how great Jesus is with words. I mean, I know He's good at everything, but He could have chosen to get His points across in a more direct or boring way. Instead, He paints us a beautiful picture, going above and beyond to draw us into what He's saying. Honestly, reading this makes me want to cry just because it's so *striking*.

> **"AND WHY DO YOU WORRY ABOUT CLOTHES? SEE HOW THE FLOWERS OF THE FIELD GROW. THEY DO NOT LABOR OR SPIN. YET I TELL YOU THAT NOT EVEN SOLOMON IN ALL HIS SPLENDOR WAS DRESSED LIKE ONE OF THESE."**
> **Matthew 6:28-29**

Imagine yourself there, sitting on that hill and listening to Jesus preach the most earth-shattering sermon you've ever heard. He begins to address your worries as if He was reading your mail. Suddenly, He points up to the sky. *Look at the birds*, He says. *Aren't you worth more?* Now He bends down and picks a flower, holding it up so you can see its vibrant colors, the beauty God wove into His creation. *Will He not clothe you even more extravagantly?*

Do you see what He's doing here? According to Jesus, the whole of creation is proof of God's love for us; it's full of signposts that our Lord cares—that He will provide what we need.

If you think about it, it's a pretty logical appeal. When we get overwhelmed or find ourselves falling into rhythms of stress and worry, it starts to feel like this up-in-the-clouds, intangible thing. Then it starts to feel impossible to overcome because we can't even grasp what it is. The feeling gets so slippery that we can't hold onto it. But Jesus brings it all back down to earth with a simple question: won't God take care of you?

03 / FIRST THINGS FIRST

Perhaps that's the secret Jesus knew. Maybe He wasn't just relying on a super, God-given self-control (though He definitely had it!), but instead He was simply trusting His Father.

Do you trust your Father? According to Jesus, that's the key! When we worry, we can remember we serve a God who has good plans for us (Jeremiah 29:11), a God that will always keep His word (Isaiah 55:11), and a God who cares about all our details (Psalm 139:13). Wow. Could it really be that simple?

Over and over, God has proven that He will take care of us—that He will come through for us. That's what Jesus is getting at with all this bird and flower talk. God has proven Himself trustworthy. He's proven that He cares. He has shown up for us time and time again. Why wouldn't He do it again?

THINK IT THROUGH!

+ REFLECT ON YOUR LIFE. WHEN HAS GOD TAKEN CARE OF YOU? WHEN HAS HE PROVEN HIMSELF TRUSTWORTHY, WHETHER IN BIG OR LITTLE WAYS?

BEAUTIFUL KINGDOM

+ LET'S TAKE SOME TIME TO PROCESS WITH THE LORD! PRAY AND EVALUATE. ARE THERE ANY AREAS OF YOUR LIFE WHERE YOU MIGHT BE BELIEVING THE LIE THAT GOD DOESN'T WANT TO COME THROUGH FOR YOU? WHAT MIGHT GOD WANT TO SAY TO YOU IN THAT UNBELIEF?

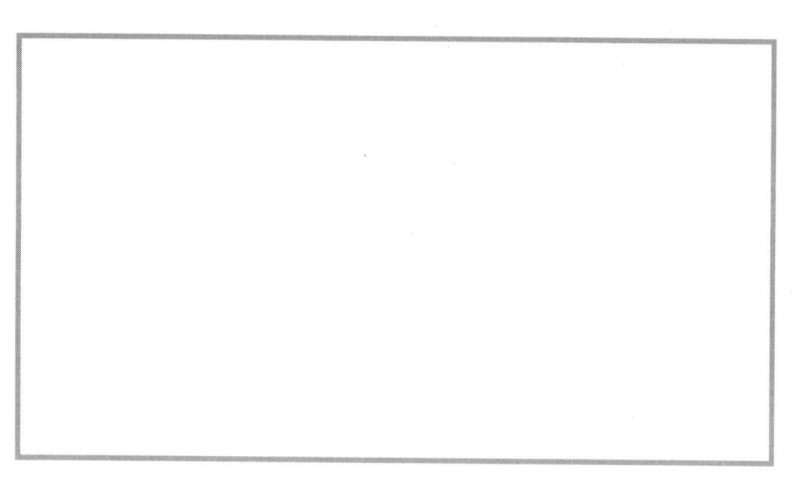

Wow. I want to camp out in this Scripture passage and never leave. So powerful! But we have to keep moving. Let's find the last portion of this week's reading.

> "BUT SEEK FIRST HIS KINGDOM AND HIS RIGHTEOUSNESS, AND ALL THESE THINGS WILL BE GIVEN TO YOU AS WELL. THEREFORE DO NOT WORRY ABOUT TOMORROW, FOR TOMORROW WILL WORRY ABOUT ITSELF. EACH DAY HAS ENOUGH TROUBLE OF ITS OWN."
> **Matthew 6:33-34**

03 / FIRST THINGS FIRST

+ LOOK BACK AT THE SCRIPTURE ON THE LAST PAGE AND CIRCLE THE WORD "FIRST."

Seek first his kingdom . . . Well, it looks like we've arrived at our last point for this week!

3. FIRST THINGS FIRST.

We're back to the Kingdom. I wasn't kidding when I said it's a running theme in the book of Matthew! The Kingdom of Heaven is clearly on Jesus's mind. And somehow, a Kingdom-focus is the antidote to worry.

Seeking the Kingdom first is the solution to the worry that plagues us. It's right there, in the words of Jesus! But what does that *mean*, and how do we apply it to our lives as college women? If the Kingdom of Heaven is God's reign breaking in (like we talked about in chapter 1) and we are called to seek it first (Matthew 6:33), how do we put it into action? Where do we go from here?

I think God gives us the answer in the book of Colossians. Check it out!

> "SINCE, THEN, YOU HAVE BEEN RAISED WITH CHRIST, SET YOUR HEARTS ON THINGS ABOVE, WHERE CHRIST IS, SEATED AT THE RIGHT HAND OF GOD. SET YOUR MINDS ON THINGS ABOVE, NOT ON EARTHLY THINGS. FOR YOU DIED, AND YOUR LIFE IS NOW HIDDEN WITH CHRIST IN GOD."
> Colossians 3:1–3, emphasis added

How do we deal with worry? We set our hearts and eyes on Jesus. *We put first things first.*

BEAUTIFUL KINGDOM

It's so simple but so profound! Jesus doesn't say that we will be free from the things that cause us to worry. In fact, He says that we will have trouble in this world (John 16:33). But we have the beautiful opportunity to fix our eyes on the One who overcame it all for us.

Why would we worry about finding the perfect outfit to impress the people around us when we have the attention of an almighty God? Why would we stress about where our next paycheck is coming from when nothing is impossible with our Father? Why would we let circumstances overwhelm us when we serve a God who has already claimed the victory on our behalf?

Jesus is inviting us to change our perspective! Here you are, staring at the mountain in front of you—overcome with fear—with no way around it. But Jesus is here. What does He do? He tilts your face up to meet His.

Look at me.

Could it be that easy? Could we really fix our eyes on Jesus and let tomorrow worry about itself? I don't know about you, but I want it to be! I want my eyes glued on my King, so sure of His plan for me that nothing will phase me or knock me off the course He has for me. But so many things try to get in the way! And if we're not careful, we'll hear a message like this and chastise ourselves for ever feeling worry. We'll tell ourselves to just try harder next time and maybe we'll be more Christlike.

Look at me.

But Jesus didn't come to your world, put on your skin, feel your feelings, take on your pain, and die your death just so you could try harder. He didn't come to shame you into submission. No! Jesus came to offer you life!

Look at me.

03 / FIRST THINGS FIRST

So this is for the woman who worries. The woman who can't pick out an outfit in the morning, the one who's terrified in social situations, the one who isn't sure if she can pay her tuition this month, the one who is desperate for an answered prayer, and the one who's anxious that she'll fall short.

Look at me.

Jesus invites you to put first things first. Look at Him. Seek His Kingdom. Tomorrow, when worry creeps in again, take that first small step toward Him. Allow Him to shift your gaze, little by little.

> **"AND ALL THESE THINGS WILL BE GIVEN TO YOU AS WELL."**
> **Matthew 6:33b**

CONVERSATION STARTERS

1. What was the last thing you found yourself worrying about? (It can be as deep or as light as you want! Just answer the first thing that comes to mind!)

2. What might it look like for God to take care of you in that area of worry?

03 / **FIRST THINGS FIRST**

3. Let's get real . . . What lies might you be believing about the character of God right now? Are there any Scriptures that replace those lies with truth?

4. What is one way you can remind yourself to keep first things first this week? Share with your group and write down any great ideas they have!

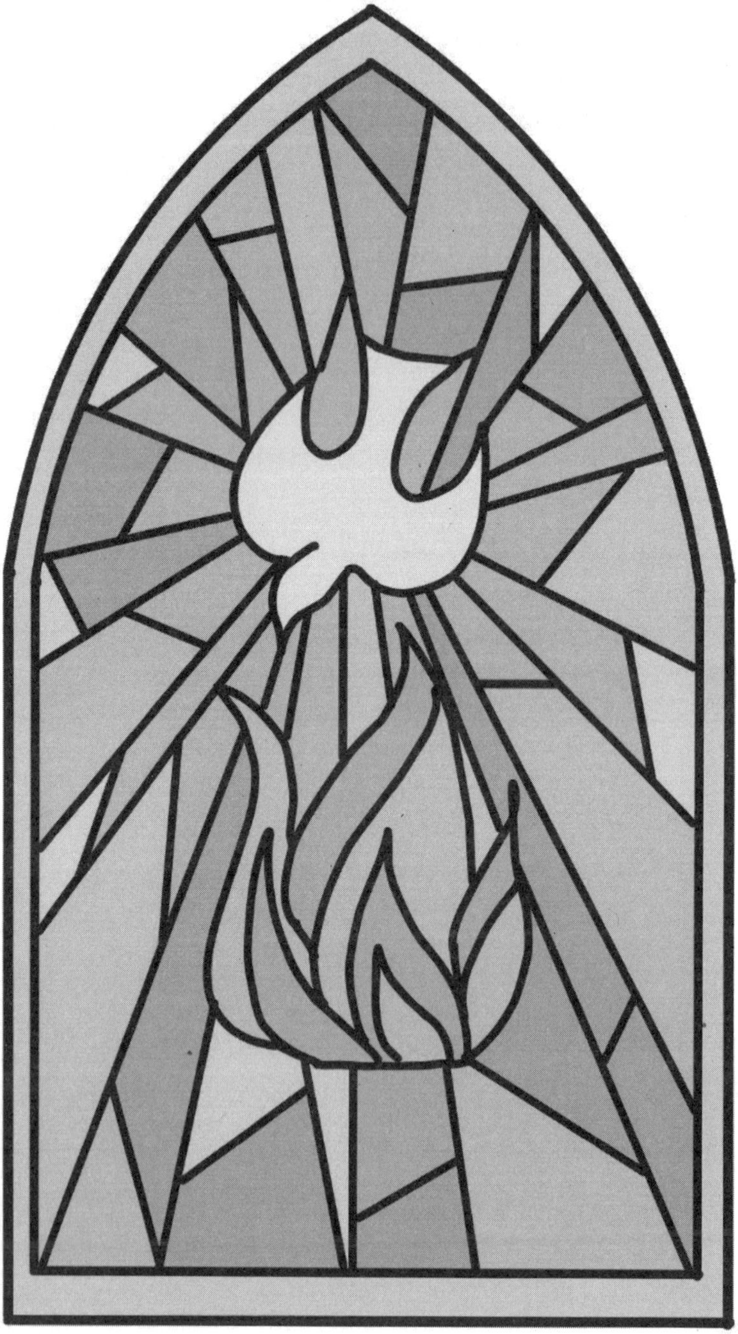

JESUS AND MESSY PEOPLE

CHAPTER 4

BEAUTIFUL KINGDOM

JESUS AND MESSY PEOPLE

Matthew 8 - 9

I want to be more like Jesus.

It's the heart cry of our Christian lives, right? *Lord, make me more like You!* It's a journey that will take a lifetime of secret moments in His presence, confession and repentance, and fires of refinement. It's what spurs us to read His Word day after day. Why else are we reading the book of Matthew other than to gaze on the beauty of Jesus and let that glow change us?

Often, when we learn more about Jesus—when we have encounters with His character and glimpses of His face—it reveals something inside of us that doesn't match. The Bible calls it "sanctification," the process of looking in the mirror at Jesus and watching our own

04 / JESUS AND MESSY PEOPLE

features change to match His. Sometimes this process is tender and smooth, a gradual etching away of walls and shells. But sometimes it feels like a stab to the heart, a quick conviction that leaves us reeling, desperate to walk like He walks and to live like He lives.

For me, the Scripture we're going to read today is a little bit of both. In this continuation of Matthew's Gospel narrative, we're going to watch Jesus interact with messy people. We're watching His compassion, His tenderness, and His utter lack of attention to social graces or cultural boundary lines as He moves toward the people the rest of us move away from. And when I see that, I'm changed a little.

First, I feel a tender nudge. *Look at that compassion*, I think. *God, would You grow that in me?* I read this Scripture and it's like I'm sitting at the table with Jesus, feeling my eyes prick with tears because I'm in awe of Him. But simultaneously, reading this Scripture hurts. Because when I watch Him reach out, I think of all the times I didn't. When I see Him love the unlovable, the messiest people, I remember when I withheld that love.

So if this chapter hurts a little, if it pokes a few rough edges or brings up something you were trying to forget, I want you to know that I'm right there with you. Our God is so sweet to draw us closer to Him, and His presence is like a blanket that covers a multitude of hurts and sins.

Our mission for this chapter (or, I guess you could say it's *God's* mission for this chapter) is to learn from Jesus. He is the kind of King who associates with the messy people, the kind of King who eats with traitors and loves the people everyone else decided were unlovable. Could we do the same? It's more than just a surface-level conversation about evangelism or reaching across social lines to invite people to church. It's a heart check. Soul surgery.

Jesus, we want to be more like You.

BEAUTIFUL KINGDOM

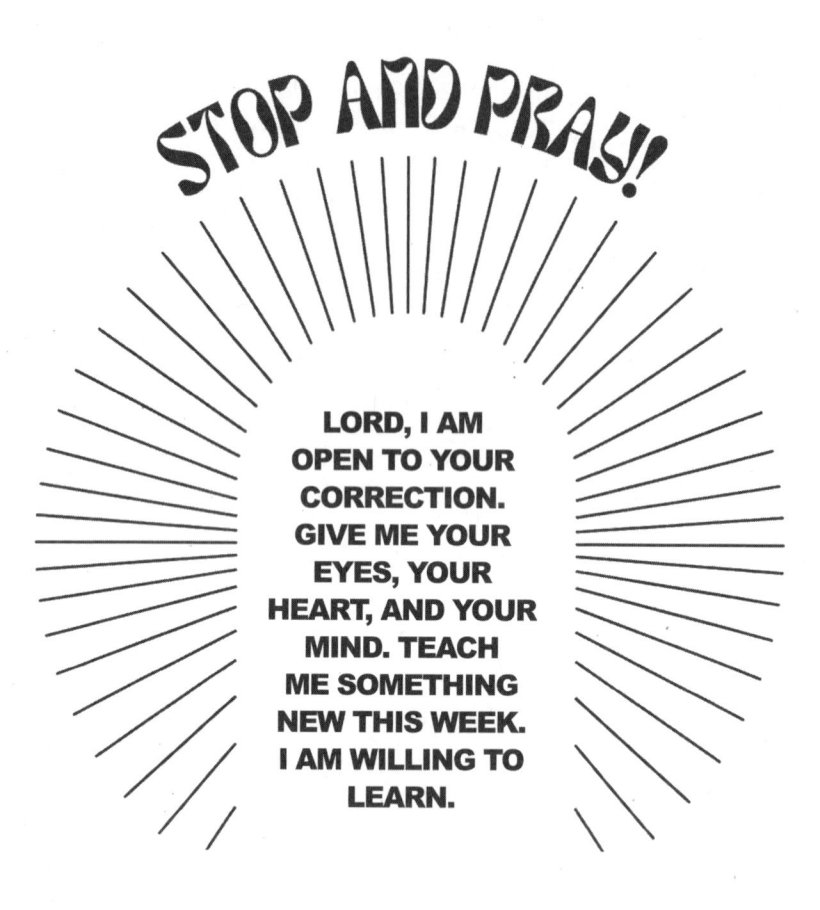

STOP AND PRAY!

LORD, I AM OPEN TO YOUR CORRECTION. GIVE ME YOUR EYES, YOUR HEART, AND YOUR MIND. TEACH ME SOMETHING NEW THIS WEEK. I AM WILLING TO LEARN.

Read Matthew 8:1–4.

+ SUMMARIZE WHAT HAPPENED IN THIS SCRIPTURE IN YOUR OWN WORDS.

We're on to the next phase in Matthew's Gospel narrative! The Sermon on the Mount is complete, Jesus has descended from the mountain, and now the next two chapters consist of ten

04 / JESUS AND MESSY PEOPLE

different miracles Jesus performed. This is Matthew's record of Jesus's "street ministry," evidence of His divinity, and proof of His character. It's the Kingdom coming to life and bursting onto the scene.

And what's the first thing Jesus does? He heals someone who's super messy.

1. JESUS'S HOLINESS IS CONTAGIOUS.

+ FILL IN THE BLANKS FROM MATTHEW 8:3.

"JESUS REACHED OUT HIS HAND AND _____ THE MAN. 'I AM WILLING,' HE SAID. 'BE CLEAN!' IMMEDIATELY HE WAS CLEANSED OF HIS LEPROSY."

OK, so this is one of those times when our distance from the ancient world and culture Jesus was living in can hinder our understanding of what's really happening. I don't know about you, but I don't encounter a lot of lepers in my day-to-day. But in Jesus's time, leprosy really was a huge problem. It wasn't just a horrible disease that disfigured the body and was super contagious, but it became embedded into their class structure; something so commonplace that it became part of the culture, requiring rules and regulations for the people who caught it.

According to Jewish customs, you had to keep at least six feet away from a leper at all times. (Whoa, maybe we can put that into our modern-day context.) If the wind was blowing you had to stay *150 feet away*. In fact, the only thing more defiling for the Jewish people in Jesus's day was to come in contact with a dead body. Yikes.[1]

By the way they followed Old Testament rules and practices, ancient Jews were thoroughly entrenched in a culture of what we could call "fragile holiness." They were set apart by God, called to be His holy people. And to maintain that holiness, they had to stay pure (i.e., staying away from things that were impure). For example, if an ancient Jew were to make contact—accidental or otherwise—with someone with leprosy, they were required to go to the temple and be purified. They were declared ceremonially unclean until the correct rights and rituals were performed. The Jews of Jesus's day wanted desperately to stay holy, but any contact with impurity would declare them unclean.

Intense, right? It sounds like a full-time job! They always had to be alert, on the lookout for anything that might defile them, leading them to live lives that were pretty separate from the non-Jews around them.

Now knowing all that, when we look back at the Scripture, it's downright *shocking*. First, just being in the vicinity of this man with leprosy was already against the rules. Then, Jesus goes as far as to *touch* him! It's wild! What is He doing? We can imagine the shock on His disciples' faces, possibly even the revulsion.

Jesus touched him. Does that mean Jesus Christ, Messiah, Son of God, was now *dirty*? Unholy? Unclean?

Well, look back at the Scripture.

> **"IMMEDIATELY HE WAS CLEANSED OF HIS LEPROSY."**
> **Matthew 8:3b**

Jesus didn't become impure by touching the man with leprosy. *The man with leprosy became pure by touching Jesus.*

04 / **JESUS AND MESSY PEOPLE**

Can you see the difference? All of the people around Him viewed their whole lives as quarantine, a desperate need to run the other way when faced with impurity. But Jesus, our loving Savior, moved *toward* the unclean people. Because only He could make them clean. His holiness wasn't fragile; it was contagious.

I love how Mark describes this moment in his Gospel account.

> **"MOVED WITH COMPASSION, JESUS REACHED OUT AND TOUCHED HIM."**
> **Mark 1:41a, NLT**

What a beautiful glimpse into the character of Jesus! He has so much compassion for the sinners and sufferers. He's not scared of our mess! Haven't we seen this to be true about Him in our own lives? How many times has He met you in your darkest moments? How many times has He run toward you when everyone else ran away? How many moments did He offer you His touch to renew your spirit?

+ CAN YOU THINK OF A TIME WHERE JESUS MET YOU IN YOUR MESS? WRITE ABOUT YOUR EXPERIENCE BELOW.

I've said this before and I'm sure I will say it again, but it's crucial that we begin our conversations with a focus on Jesus and His character. Before we even begin to explore what our hearts should be for the broken and forgotten, we have to know what Jesus's heart is for them. He's the best starting point! And according to what we read in Matthew, Jesus—out of compassion—moves toward the people others move away from.

2. JESUS MOVES TOWARD MESSY PEOPLE.

Let's fast-forward in the Scripture a little bit to find another moment when Jesus gave us a glimpse of His heart for messy people.

Read Matthew 9:9–13.

Matthew! Ahhhh! This is the moment where our author records his own calling from Jesus. How cool that we get an inside look!

> "AS JESUS WENT ON FROM THERE, HE SAW A MAN NAMED MATTHEW SITTING AT THE TAX COLLECTOR'S BOOTH. 'FOLLOW ME,' HE TOLD HIM, AND MATTHEW GOT UP AND FOLLOWED HIM."
> **Matthew 9:9**

We already learned in chapter 1 that Matthew was a tax collector. Though he was born a Jew, Matthew worked for the Roman Empire. His whole job was to tax his own people, often with unfair rates—as you would expect from a conquering nation. So, obviously, those with his job title were not well liked around town.

04 / JESUS AND MESSY PEOPLE

Jesus calling Matthew to His side would have been as shocking as your university hiring an eight year old to teach an economics class. It was weird. It didn't make sense. And as we keep on reading, Jesus takes it a step further and goes to a dinner party with the worst of the worst.

Unexpected kingdom? Definitely.

Predictably, the religious leaders were a little peeved and a lot confused by Jesus's actions. If He was claiming to be the Messiah, the holiest of holies, why was He eating with the dirtiest of sinners? And Jesus's response rocks our world just as much now as it must have for the first people who heard it.

+ FILL IN THE BLANKS FROM MATTHEW 9:12–13.

**"ON HEARING THIS, JESUS SAID, 'IT IS NOT THE _____ WHO NEED A DOCTOR, BUT THE _____. BUT GO AND LEARN WHAT THIS MEANS: "I DESIRE MERCY, NOT SACRIFICE." FOR I HAVE NOT COME TO CALL THE _____, BUT _____."'
MATTHEW 9:12–13**

We've all sinned and fallen short of the glory of God. Thank the Lord that Jesus chose to seek us out. Jesus Christ, friend of sinners.

It reminds me of this quote from one of my favorite books about Jesus...

The cumulative testimony of the four Gospels is that when Jesus Christ sees the fallenness of the world all about him, his deepest impulse, his most natural instinct, is to move toward that sin and suffering, not away from it.
Dane C. Ortlund, Gentle and Lowly[2]

BEAUTIFUL KINGDOM

Now, there is something important to note here. Yes, Jesus hung out with some bad influences. Well, He more than hung out with them; He actively sought them out, always seeking to get in rooms with them. *But, Jesus didn't change Himself when He was with them.* His purpose was to heal them, to bring light to their dark places. He didn't dim Himself to fit in. Instead, He invited them to live as He did.

When we really take to heart that Jesus moved toward broken people, we are bound to feel called to do the same. And I think we should! (We're going to talk more about it in a little bit.) But this comes with a huge thing to remember: you can't march into messy places and start acting like them. You are called to be a light in the dark. That means you're going to look a little different.

I was talking through this Scripture with a friend the other day and she shared her own story with me. In college, when she first began to explore her faith, she thought she could be the "cool Christian." She would lead a Bible study on Wednesday nights then go out with her friends on Friday so she could prove to them she wasn't judgemental. But over time, she realized she wasn't really representing Jesus to them. Instead, she was letting her faith fall to the wayside because their way of living looked more attractive in those moments.

I believe this Scripture is going to call us into unknown territory to seek and save the lost. But first, you have to be sure of where you stand. Find good heart-friends who hold you accountable and lead you closer to Jesus. Establish your faith on the rock of Jesus Christ, seeking to know Him more every day. Then, as an overflow, you can be sent.

> **SIDE NOTE . . .**
> Are you unsure if you're standing on a firm foundation with Jesus? We are so glad you're reading this book! We'll dive even deeper into what a life with Jesus looks like next week.

Does that make sense? OK! Then let's get sent! Here's the question

04 / JESUS AND MESSY PEOPLE

we should all ask ourselves: Jesus moved toward messy people—but *do I?*

Sometimes I wonder if the more entrenched we become in Christian culture, the more distant we become from the people who need Christ. Under the banner of living set apart (which is an important Biblical calling!) we begin to shun others who we feel aren't on our level, whether intentionally or unintentionally.

I don't know what it looks like for you, but I've been guilty of this time and time again. When I stopped drinking, I started to look down on my friends who did drink, thinking they just weren't as far along in their faith as I was. I've held back from inviting a friend to Delight because I assumed she wouldn't fit in. I've ditched "bad influence" friends who may have needed the light of Jesus I had in me.

Jesus offers us a better way to live, a way to look a little more like Him. Don't you want to take that invitation? I know I do!

THINK IT THROUGH!

+ DO YOU HAVE GOD-FEARING FRIENDS IN YOUR LIFE WHO HOLD YOU ACCOUNTABLE? WHAT ARE THEY LIKE? IF NOT, WHERE MIGHT YOU LOOK TO FIND THEM?

+ LET'S GET SUPER HONEST . . . DO YOU MOVE TOWARD MESSY PEOPLE OR AWAY FROM THEM? ARE THERE ANY AREAS IN YOUR LIFE WHERE YOU'VE BEEN CLOSED OFF, JUDGEMENTAL, OR MISSED AN OPPORTUNITY TO SHARE JESUS OUT OF FEAR? RECORD YOUR STREAM OF CONSCIOUSNESS BELOW.

Wow, I'm starting to get excited! Our hearts are already changing, being formed and reformed in His image. Jesus has a beautiful invitation in store for us that I believe will energize our spirits and motivate our hearts! Let's dive back into Scripture to find it.

> "JUST THEN A WOMAN WHO HAD BEEN SUBJECT TO BLEEDING FOR TWELVE YEARS CAME UP BEHIND HIM AND TOUCHED THE EDGE OF HIS CLOAK. SHE SAID TO HERSELF, 'IF I ONLY TOUCH HIS CLOAK, I WILL BE HEALED.' JESUS TURNED AND SAW HER. 'TAKE HEART, DAUGHTER,' HE SAID, 'YOUR FAITH HAS HEALED YOU.' AND THE WOMAN WAS HEALED AT THAT MOMENT."
>
> **Matthew 9:20-22**

Here's where it's all been heading: all it takes is one touch.

04 / JESUS AND MESSY PEOPLE

3. JUST ONE TOUCH.

This bleeding woman was another example of an "impure" character. She would have been shunned to the fringes of society, unable to have physical contact with anybody, ever. And boy was she desperate for healing. In her need and by faith, she reached out and touched Jesus's robe. And she was made *clean*, just like the leper.

I would say that a lot of us can buy into this truth, that just one touch from Jesus can change everything. Maybe we've experienced it in our own lives when we first found soul-rescue in His arms, when we watched a friend be freed from anxiety during a worship night, or when we heard someone share a radical testimony of life-change. But what about the tax collectors? The messy people? The people we've decided are too far gone?

Could one touch save them, too?

There is something deep in our human nature that loves to put people in boxes. We know that God saved us, but we have trouble believing He would save the people we feel are less than us. Just like the Pharisees couldn't see past a tax-collector job title, we struggle to see past certain political affiliations, certain bad habits, or certain personality traits. Subconsciously, we begin to think we're better than they are, that we deserved what we got.

But here's the thing! Nobody deserves what Jesus offers. You and I are just as much of a mess as the people we're scared of. Our Jesus came to seek and save the *lost*. We aren't excluded from that category! And maybe it's that simple reminder of our own need for rescue that can soften our hearts to the others who need the same.

Now here's where it gets exciting. If all it takes is one touch from Jesus to radically turn a life upside down, to purify a heart, then maybe we get to be the vessel for that touch.

BEAUTIFUL KINGDOM

+ FIND 2 CORINTHIANS 5:20 AND COPY IT DOWN IN THE SPACE BELOW.

We are Christ's ambassadors! He chose you and I to be the bearers of His healing touch to a world in need! What an honor! And to do that, we need to stop quarantining ourselves off in fear of contagion. You see, when Jesus died on the cross as the perfect sacrifice, He gave us His righteousness. We're now carriers of His holiness, made pure by His blood in a way that is nowhere near fragile. We are called to step into the dark places armed with the confidence that the God of angel armies is on our side. Through the power of the Spirit in us, we *get* to activate our faith! We *get* to bring the name of Jesus to the ends of the earth!

What might that look like for you? Does it mean going on coffee dates with people you'd previously excluded? Does it mean going to new parts of campus, talking to that one girl in class, or serving in a ministry reaching out to the broken?

+ LET'S BRAINSTORM! WHAT WOULD IT LOOK LIKE TO BE CHRIST'S AMBASSADOR IN YOUR COMMUNITY?

04 / JESUS AND MESSY PEOPLE

Now, I want to speak to the girl who feels like she's still "messy." The girl who doesn't feel welcome in church settings, the girl who's been cut off one too many times, the girl who wonders if she really is too far gone.

Jesus's healing touch applies to you, too. There is no such thing as "too far gone" in the beautiful Kingdom Jesus came to usher in. You can decide, today, to receive His restorative love. You can choose today to walk with Him in confidence, to breathe in His new life. And then you can turn around to your friends in those dark places and reach out your hand.

Do you see it? I see the love of Jesus spreading like wildfire on the shoulders of bold women who know what He did for them. I see even the most unlikely people being welcomed into holy places with open arms. I see the Great Commission bursting to life.

It's soaking into our hearts now, correcting us, changing us, opening our eyes a little wider so we can meditate on the beauty of Jesus and His character, His compassion. Jesus broke down barriers and upset the status quo to reach out to the people who were unreachable. Then, He empowered us to do the same.

Here we are, Jesus. Send us!

BEAUTIFUL KINGDOM

CONVERSATION STARTERS

1. After reading this Scripture, do you feel like God is teaching you something new or revealing something in your heart? What is it?

2. If you're being honest, what has been your knee-jerk reaction when faced with "messy" people? Maybe fear, judgment, compassion or lack thereof, indifference? Process your thoughts below.

04 / **JESUS AND MESSY PEOPLE**

3. We believe that God can soften our hearts toward others. Is there anyone He is bringing to mind this week that you feel led to pursue?

4. Let's put this into action! In your group, exchange ideas for how we can be Christ's ambassadors this week and pursue even the messiest people. (Jot down your favorite ideas below.)

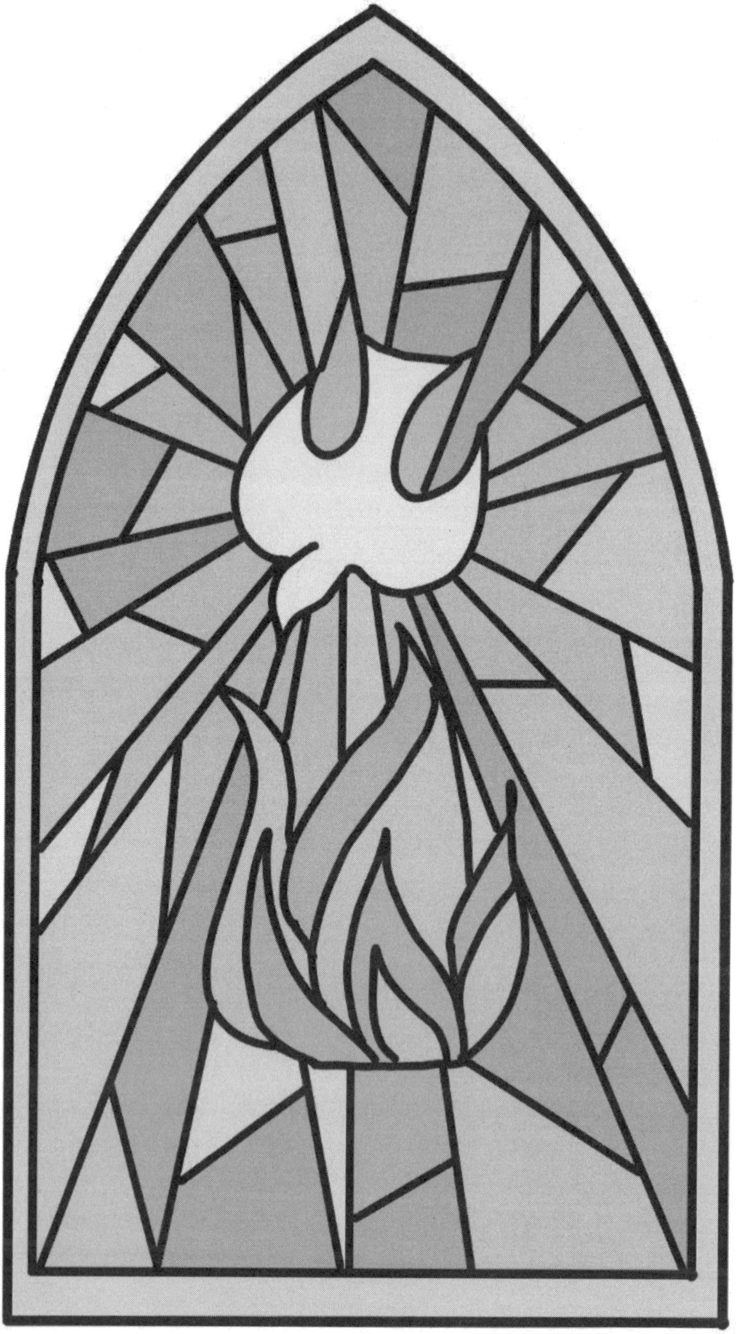

COME TO ME

CHAPTER 5

BEAUTIFUL KINGDOM

COME TO ME

Matthew 11:28 - 30

I figured out at a young age that just being myself wasn't enough. If I wanted people to like me I needed to be *more*. More energetic. More charismatic. More memorable. More self-sacrificing. More interesting. More unique. I dropped the real me like she was a shell I could shed, putting on new versions of myself designed to win the favor of the people around me instead.

For my elementary school friends I became wild, someone they could joke around and have a good laugh with. For my middle school friends I became a flirt, the girl who could hang with the boys and always leave them wanting more. For my high school friends I became the Goody Two-shoes, the girl who hid the fact that she couldn't connect with others by pretending that she didn't even want to—that she was above it all. For my college friends I became the giver, the girl who would always be there, ready to give the best advice for anyone who needed it. Even now, I wonder what

05 / COME TO ME

shell I'm wearing, who I'm trying to be to earn affection, attention, or a sense of belonging.

Has that been my life then? Trying, trying, trying, and trying but never quite attaining that restful state of acceptance? Never finding that calm belonging I was craving? Every desperate try, every new shell of a person, is like another rock on my shoulders weighing me down, down, down.

Well, has that been your life? Do you find yourself trying, trying, trying, and trying but never feeling like you did enough? Maybe you didn't have to work so hard to fit in, but you tried for good grades, for validation from your parents, to find a husband, to achieve a certain job title, to chase a certain dream.

Aren't you sick of trying so hard? Are you sick of the heaviness it brings? I know I am. We get this bone-deep weariness as we keep looking for new heights to soar to, never acknowledging a place to land. And I wonder . . . Do we treat our faith that way?

Are we trying, trying, trying for God's affection?

Are we trying, trying, trying to feel like we've actually secured our spot in Heaven?

Are we trying, trying, trying to be known as the Christian girl?

Are we trying, trying, trying to stop doubting, to finally know all the answers?

Are we trying, trying, trying to deserve God's love?

I'm dedicating this chapter to us: the women who feel heavy. The women who are tired of trying so hard. I can picture Jesus sitting right next to each and every one of us. He has His hand stretched out, ready to invite us into something real and true and *light*.

Finally.

STOP AND PRAY!

GOD, I DON'T WANT TO BEAR THIS WEIGHT ANY LONGER. I INVITE YOU IN TODAY. I KNOW I CAN'T DO THIS WITHOUT YOU.

This week we're going to read three verses from Matthew. That's right! Only three. Think of it like an invitation for God to reveal Himself, especially for us girls who wear our intense Scripture reading and study skills like a badge on our chests. Do we believe that God's big enough to speak to us—to radically change our lives—in just three verses? Are just a few sentences from His mouth enough?

I'll go ahead and spoil the ending: Yes, it is enough. *He* is enough. So let's read.

+ READ MATTHEW 11:28–30 AND COPY IT DOWN ON THE NEXT PAGE. (WE ENCOURAGE YOU TO WRITE THE

05 / COME TO ME

WHOLE THING OUT! IT'S NOT TOO LONG!)

We're going to take this Scripture piece by piece and see what God has in store for us. I believe He has an invitation for all of us—the women who feel heavy, the women who are desperate, the women who are sick of trying so hard. And what's that invitation? *Come to me.*

1. COME TO ME.

> **"COME TO ME, ALL YOU WHO ARE WEARY AND BURDENED, AND I WILL GIVE YOU REST."**
> **Matthew 11:28**

When was the last time you received a good, quality hug? Honestly I'm not much of a hugger, but when I'm feeling sad, it's exactly what I need. I can think of so many times when I was on the verge of tears and my husband, my mom, or a friend would just stand there and open their arms, an invitation for me to get some comfort and cry on their shoulder.

That's what this verse reminds me of. I wonder if when Jesus first spoke these words, He had His arms out like that. Open, ready to receive. Earlier in Matthew, He spoke of the people of Israel as "weary and helpless" (Matthew 9:36, TPT). He had so much compassion on His hurting children, so maybe He knew they needed His embrace. I think if I had been there, I would have taken Him up on that offer. He's probably the best hugger.

You see, Jesus is asking something of us here. "Come to me," He says. It's an action that would require something from us, a few steps of effort on our part. And for so many years, I read this verse as a marching order. I'd see it as a reprimand. *Oh, I'm feeling weary and burdened? I guess I should have come to Jesus and I wouldn't be feeling this way.* But that's just not even close to what He means. His "Come to me" is like that hug, an invitation for us to run to His arms like a child, not a criticism for letting ourselves stray outside of His grip.

Because no matter how hard we try to appear otherwise, we are the weary and burdened people He's calling to His arms. He's talking to us who are exhausted from trying to earn His love. *Come to me.* He's talking to us who feel overwhelmed by the weight of unconfessed sin. *Come to me.* He's even talking to those who've spent their whole lives running the other direction, who've never felt His embrace. *Come to me.*

But it is a step. It's humbling to admit a need for Jesus; it's hard to admit you can't do it on your own. Stepping toward Jesus means stepping away from old ways of living, away from the sin patterns you're stuck in, away from habits you're not sure if you want to shake, away from self-satisfaction. But the *rest* He offers at the end is worth it. Because we've been trying on our own for so long and we haven't been able to find that rest. Turning to Jesus is our only option.

+ WHAT ARE YOU WEARY FROM OR BURDENED BY IN THIS SEASON?

05 / COME TO ME

WHAT IS MAKING YOU DESPERATE FOR A HUG FROM JESUS RIGHT NOW? PROCESS YOUR THOUGHTS AND FEELINGS BELOW.

I know it might feel like we're jumping right into the really vulnerable stuff, but I don't think we need any fluff this week. Jesus wants to invite us into His rest, a better way to live our lives than what we've been doing. And isn't that such a picture of His beautiful Kingdom? Jesus says through the prophet in the book of Revelation, "Here I am! I stand at the door and knock. If anyone hears my voice and opens the door, I will come in and eat with that person, and they with me" (Revelation 3:20). This is an open invitation, outstretched arms for all who are desperate for Him, all who are in need of His rest.

But why do we wait so long to accept that invitation? Why do we leave Him knocking and knocking instead of opening the door and welcoming Him in? I wonder if it's because we've let our circumstances teach us lies about Who we're letting in. Maybe we don't trust that what Jesus has to offer really is better than what we've got, burdens and all.

Jesus answers that fear in the next verse.

BEAUTIFUL KINGDOM

> "TAKE MY YOKE UPON YOU AND LEARN FROM ME, FOR I AM GENTLE AND HUMBLE IN HEART, AND YOU WILL FIND REST FOR YOUR SOULS."
> Matthew 11:29

2. JESUS IS GENTLE AND HUMBLE.

This verse is monumental in more ways than one. For its original audience, they would have immediately understood the farming connection He implies with all the "yoke" talk. For us, it may seem a little more out of the box. (Honestly, I have a friend who went years thinking this verse was talking about egg yolks. Anyone else?) In a nutshell, a yoke is what was used to string two oxen together so they could plow a field. So in a way, this is another invitation from Jesus. *Yoke up with me*, He says. *Drop your old yokes! Mine is better!* I encourage you to do your own deep dive into all the implications of this metaphor because it's awesome.

TAKE IT DEEPER . . .
Here's what a yoke looks like! Cool, right?

But in this season of my life, I'm even more moved by what He threw in right in the middle. Did you miss it? Here, Jesus chooses to describe His heart, the only time in all the Gospels that He does this. And how does He describe Himself?

Gentle and humble.

05 / COME TO ME

A few years ago, my mother-in-law added her credit card onto my Starbucks app. (Hang in there. This is going to make sense in a minute.) Every once in a while, she would text me and tell me to get a coffee on her because she was thinking of me. As time passed, I started to reach out to her and ask if I could use it on days when money was tight or when I left my card at home. Every time I asked, she *always* said yes. Eventually, I started to just use it when I needed it because I knew what she'd say. I knew that she was generous to her core and that she loved to give me that gift, so I confidently partook in those little Starbucks blessings.

I knew her character, so I approached her with confidence. Do you think the same principle can apply to our relationship with Jesus? Maybe we leave Him knocking because we worry that when we let Him in and He sees our mess—how weary and burdened we really are—that He'll respond harshly, with condemnation, or maybe even indifference.

But Jesus says that He is gentle and humble. So what does that mean for us?

It means that we can confidently accept his open-arms invitation because we know, for sure and without a doubt, how He will respond. He will treat us gently. He will get down low with us, unafraid of our mess.

It reminds me of a parable Jesus shared in the book of Luke. Check it out!

+ READ LUKE 15:11–32 AND SUMMARIZE IT IN YOUR OWN WORDS IN THE SPACE BELOW.

The father in the story (meant to represent God) had been given the cold shoulder by his son. The boy had forsaken his father's love, demanded his money, then run off for greener pastures, confident he could do life without his dad. Then, when he realized he really couldn't do it on his own, he came crawling back, penniless and weary. By all rights, the father should have been angry. He should have demanded the son pay him back what he owed or forced him to become a servant in his household. But what did the father do?

> **"BUT WHILE HE WAS STILL A LONG WAY OFF, HIS FATHER SAW HIM AND WAS FILLED WITH COMPASSION FOR HIM; HE RAN TO HIS SON, THREW HIS ARMS AROUND HIM AND KISSED HIM."**
> **Luke 15:20**

The father responded with *compassion*. Humbly, he allowed his son back in. Gently, he clothed him in a new robe.

Could that be God's heart for you, too? What if all this time you've been running—desperate to clean yourself up for Him or convinced He wouldn't want you anyway—He's actually been standing on the front porch waiting for you? What if He sees you now, a long way off, and runs toward you? What if He wants to welcome you with open arms and restore you, regardless of your past?

If your soul needs rest, Jesus promises to provide it.

+ WHAT DO YOU THINK HAS BEEN HOLDING YOU BACK FROM COMING TO JESUS WITH YOUR BURDENS? WRITE IT ON THE NEXT PAGE.

05 / COME TO ME

One more verse. Let's read it.

> **"FOR MY YOKE IS EASY AND MY BURDEN IS LIGHT."**
> **Matthew 11:30**

+ LOOK BACK AT THE VERSE ABOVE AND CIRCLE "LIGHT."

3. FINALLY LIGHT.

I want to tell you something I wish someone had told me during all those years of trying and trying. *You don't have to feel this way.*

That weight on your shoulders? It's not meant to be there. Your Savior is a *burden lifter*. He offers you His shoulders to share. He can bear the weight. You don't have to hold it a second longer.

But why? Why is His yoke—friendship with Him and submission to His authority—easy? Why is His burden light? Why can we just give Him our burdens? How does that change things?

This isn't some magical or willy-nilly trust exercise. This isn't a state of mind we're trying to manifest or a discipline we can learn if we try hard enough. His yoke is easy and His burden is light because Jesus Christ took the burden of the cross on His shoulders when He died on Calvary. Jesus bore the weight of every single burden, the weight of every sin and hurt. He *died* so you wouldn't have to feel this way!

You see, He knew you could never rescue yourself. He saw you crumbling under that weight. And He chose to take it for you, to bear the weight of the world on His shoulders so that you could be *light*. His offer is for us to die to ourselves—the part of us that hurts, that's caught in a web of sin, that's tired and beaten down, that wants to do it on our own—and to take up His cross. That's His yoke! It's light because He already paid the price.

You can stop living under the burdens Jesus died for. You can feel light, finally.

+ FIND GALATIANS 5:1 AND FILL IN THE BLANKS BELOW.

"IT IS FOR _____ THAT CHRIST HAS SET US FREE. STAND FIRM, THEN, AND DO NOT LET YOURSELVES BE _____ AGAIN BY A _____ OF _____." GALATIANS 5:1

You've been set free. Those chains are gone! Now we get to step into the fullness of what He has for us.

I don't know what it looks like for you to surrender your burdens to the burden lifter. Maybe you've been crushed under the pressure to perform and He wants to take that from you and offer you His affirmation that isn't based on your effort. Maybe you've been stuck in a cycle of sin and shame and He wants to unlock

05 / COME TO ME

repentance in your heart so you can experience freedom. Maybe you've never given your life to Him, never accepted the gift of the cross, and He's calling you now to lay your life down so He can make you new.

Whatever it is, I want to encourage you to take that step. He will wait forever, but why make Him wait when freedom—*lightness*—is knocking at the door? Your time can be now! He says, "Come to me." You can say yes.

THINK IT THROUGH!

+ HOW DO YOU FEEL CALLED TO RESPOND TO GOD'S INVITATION THIS WEEK?

BEAUTIFUL KINGDOM

+ IMAGINE . . . WHAT WOULD FREEDOM AND LIGHTNESS LOOK LIKE IN YOUR LIFE? HOW WOULD THINGS CHANGE FOR YOU IF YOU ACCEPTED HIS INVITATION?

I'm overwhelmed with gratitude for a Savior who welcomes us with open arms. He loves us when we don't deserve it, He shoulders the burdens of the messes we make, and He actually enjoys our company. What kind of love is this!? Today, take God's invitation to step into His beautiful Kingdom.

We've been set free.

Finally.

05 / COME TO ME

BEAUTIFUL KINGDOM

CONVERSATION STARTERS

We're going to do things a little differently this week! Go ahead and answer question #1 on your own time. Then, we will engage with the rest together in our Delight Weekly Gatherings! (If you are doing this study on your own, we encourage you to go all in with this prayer time! We believe God has something in store for you.)

1. Matthew 11:28–30 is super popular in Christian circles! Did you see it in a new way after reading this chapter, or did a specific portion of it stand out to you? How so?

OK, now let's take some time to COME TO JESUS! (Group Prayer Activity)

2. What burden are you feeling called to bring to Jesus this week? Maybe it's trying to do life on your own, stress about school, a secret sin pattern, or an unrealized dream. Or, maybe there's something you know you probably should bring to Him but you don't want to . . . Whatever it is, write it down.

05 / COME TO ME

Now, if you're ready, pray as a group to surrender your burdens at His feet!

3. How does God respond to what you've brought Him? In prayer, does any Bible verse, picture, or feeling come to mind? We know that Jesus is humble and gentle at heart. What would it look like for Him to treat you humbly and gently in that area?

Take some time to sit with the Lord then share your thoughts with your group.

4. When we come to Jesus, He takes our burdens and offers us *lightness* and *freedom* in return. Process what your heart went through while engaging with this Scripture and during prayer time. Do you feel any different? How might your life look different moving forward?

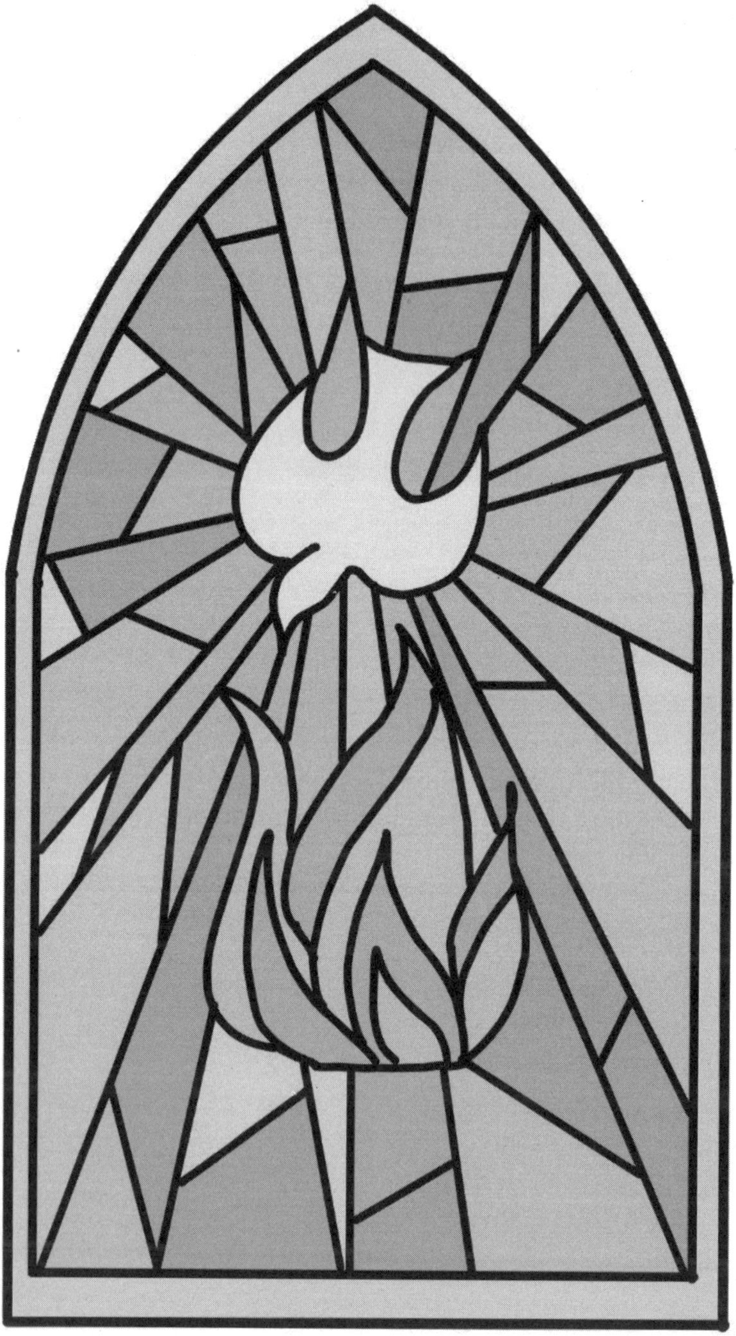

WHEN JESUS CALLS YOU OUT

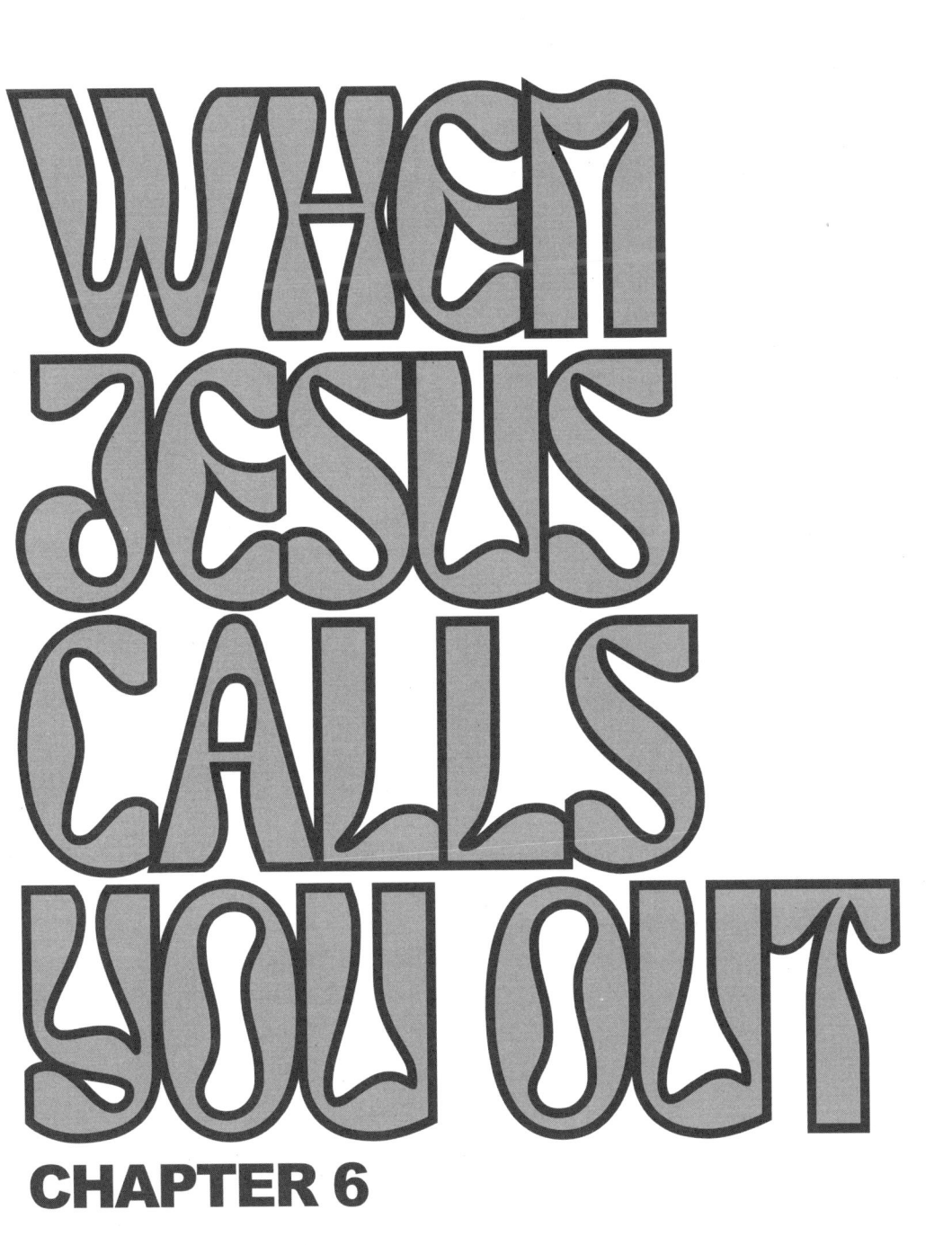

CHAPTER 6

BEAUTIFUL KINGDOM

WHEN JESUS CALLS YOU OUT

Matthew 16:21 – 28

I'm not quite sure how it happened, but somehow we're already on *chapter six* of our Matthew study. Over halfway through? No way! Our prayer is that throughout the past five weeks, you've drawn a little bit closer to the heart of God, seen your Savior a little bit clearer, and gotten a little bit more excited about the beautiful Kingdom Jesus came to announce. Thank you, God, for showing up!

+ REFLECT ON THE LAST FIVE CHAPTERS OF THIS STUDY. HOW HAS GOD SHOWN UP FOR YOU THROUGH HIS WORD? HAVE YOU LEARNED ANYTHING

06 / WHEN JESUS CALLS YOU OUT

NEW ABOUT HIM, YOURSELF, OR THE KINGDOM?

So much has happened between Matthew 11 (where Jesus invited us to come to Him) and Matthew 16 (where we're landing this week). Jesus preached a lot of amazing messages, told a lot of parables, lost His cousin John, miraculously fed five thousand people *and* four thousand people, walked on water, and performed many more miracles. You're going to want to read it, ladies! We encourage you to put some time on your calendar this week to go back through and check it out.

Our home base for this week is Matthew 16:21–28. Go ahead and read it!

+ JOT DOWN ANY PARTS THAT STOOD OUT TO YOU FROM MATTHEW 16:21–28.

BEAUTIFUL KINGDOM

Not so warm and fluffy, right? This week we're going to talk about correction: what to do when Jesus calls you out. This Scripture will address our pride and call us deeper into humility and submission under our Father. If that doesn't sound too exciting, don't worry! I believe God has freedom for us here, something jubilant and life-giving.

When I think of God's correction in my own life, one particular story comes to mind. A few years ago, I was feeling pretty slighted and passed over. There was this opportunity for greater leadership that I really wanted and when I didn't get it, I became a little bit grumpy. It felt unfair! I had so much to offer . . . Why wasn't I being used in a greater capacity?

Yeah, we can see the problem in my thought patterns already.

During that season, I received a random phone call from an old mentor of mine who I had fallen out of touch with. She called out of the blue and, as we caught up, I told her about the situation and how I was feeling. She got quiet for a second and then said . . .

Actually, I think God wants me to tell you something about that. It's why I called.

She told me that I had come to her mind as she was listening to a podcast about Christian leaders who had gained a large following and platform at a young age, then had run off the rails—crashed and burned, you could say. She said that it had made her think of me. (Oof, gut punch!)

God isn't giving you this opportunity because you aren't ready for it yet, she said. *If you were to have that level of influence right now, it would cause you to stumble. He's protecting you by saying no.*

Talk about correction! Let me tell you, that was a hard pill to swallow. Nobody wants to be told they aren't ready or that they aren't spiritually mature enough to handle something. But I can say with 100 percent certainty that I needed to hear that from her.

06 / WHEN JESUS CALLS YOU OUT

She was delivering a message straight from the Lord! And that phone call changed so much for me. As crazy as it sounds, her correction led me to freedom. After that conversation (and some desperate prayer), I was no longer trapped in a cycle of frustration. I knew what God's plan was for me and I knew what my course was supposed to be. I could rest in His guidance instead of feeling rest*less* in all my grumpiness and doubt.

So you see, God's correction is good. And a guy named Peter, one of Jesus's disciples, learned that same lesson thousands of years ago—straight from the mouth of Jesus.

Let's get some background on Peter! Jesus called him straight out of his fishing boat to fish for people all the way back in Matthew 4. He's widely regarded as one of Jesus's closest buddies and also one of Jesus's most *hot-headed* followers. He's this larger-than-life character who makes us feel a little bit better about being a tiny bit wild sometimes. If Jesus could love Peter unconditionally, He can love us, too!

Right before our reading in Matthew 16, Peter had a pretty huge moment. Check it out!

Read Matthew 16:13–20.

Did you catch what just happened there? Peter, hot-headed and wild as he was, got to be the first to openly and confidently name Jesus as the Messiah. And Jesus was so pumped about it that He renamed him. Formerly known as Simon, Peter was now the rock on which Jesus would build His church. This moment is so significant. What an honor!

But what does Peter do immediately after this holy moment? He gets a little too sure of himself.

+ FILL IN THE BLANKS FROM MATTHEW 16:21–22 ON THE NEXT PAGE.

> "FROM THAT TIME ON JESUS BEGAN TO EXPLAIN TO HIS DISCIPLES THAT HE MUST GO TO JERUSALEM AND SUFFER MANY THINGS AT THE HANDS OF THE ELDERS, THE CHIEF PRIESTS AND THE TEACHERS OF THE LAW, AND THAT HE MUST BE KILLED AND ON THE THIRD DAY BE RAISED TO LIFE. _____ TOOK HIM ASIDE AND BEGAN TO _____ HIM. 'NEVER, LORD!' HE SAID. 'THIS SHALL _____ HAPPEN TO YOU!'"

Right after being publically blessed and favored by Jesus, pride sneaks into Peter's heart.

1. PRIDE IS SNEAKY.

Reading this verse is kind of shocking; we can't even believe that Peter has the guts to say that to Jesus, especially right after he acknowledged Jesus as *God*. He tries to correct Jesus; he rebukes Him! The Greek word there for "rebuked" is *epitimao*, which means to reprove or censure. It's a harsh word! In fact, it's the same word used throughout the Gospels to describe the way Jesus talks to demons that have possessed people.

So, uh, what's going on, Peter?

What's happening here in Peter's heart is pride: that feeling when we get too sure of ourselves or when we inflate our own perception of ourselves up and up and up. Right after being praised by Jesus, Peter probably felt like he was on cloud nine! But he didn't check himself—too caught up in the moment—and ended up thinking he knew more than Jesus.

It's easy to read this and just brush Peter off as dumb.

06 / WHEN JESUS CALLS YOU OUT

I would never speak to Jesus like that, we think. *I would never try to correct God!* But if you think about it, we do the same thing all the time, whether we realize it or not.

Our pride leads us to disobedience, thinking we are above a command or guideline in the Bible. We look God in the eyes and tell Him we don't think what He said is all that important.

Our pride leads us to judgmentalness, calling out sins we see in our friends lives while ignoring our own brokenness. We tell Jesus that He didn't really need to die for us, just them.

Our pride leads us to wrong decisions, stepping out in self-confidence instead of faith. We tell the Holy Spirit we know the way instead of asking Him where we should walk.

+ WHERE HAS PRIDE SHOWN UP IN YOUR LIFE? WHERE DO YOU THINK IT MIGHT BE SNEAKING IN RIGHT NOW?

So maybe we can empathize with Peter a little bit! Because I don't know about you, but I wonder if I would have said the same thing if I were in his position. Jesus, his best friend and Savior, just said He was going to *die*. We can understand the harsh reaction!

That's why pride is so dangerous! It sneaks up on us, flowing freely out of us when we least expect it and taking root in shadowed, forgotten parts of our hearts. And I think the first step to finding freedom from it is acknowledging that it's there, bringing it to the light. The Bible says that if you say you have no sin, you deceive yourself (1 John 1:8). We are so done walking around deceived! Pride has snuck its way into all of our hearts, just like it did for Peter. Once we identify it, we can allow the Lord to free us from it.

Knowing all that, Jesus's reaction makes a lot more sense.

+ FILL IN THE BLANKS FROM MATTHEW 16:23.

"JESUS TURNED AND SAID TO PETER, '_____ _____ _____, _____! YOU ARE A STUMBLING BLOCK TO ME; YOU DO NOT HAVE IN MIND THE CONCERNS OF _____, BUT MERELY _____ CONCERNS.'"

We have to admit . . . This comes off pretty harsh. Does that confuse you? We learned last week that Jesus is humble and gentle. Why is He being harsh with Peter?

This is a great opportunity to lean into what we know to be true! We know that Jesus *is* humble and gentle—good to His core. So that must mean that His correction to Peter here—His rebuke to his rebuke—is *good*.

2. CORRECTION IS GOOD.

Does the phrasing Jesus is using here ring any bells? If you've been reading along through Matthew, it might!

+ FIND MATTHEW 4:10 AND COPY IT DOWN IN THE SPACE ON THE NEXT PAGE.

06 / WHEN JESUS CALLS YOU OUT

Right after His baptism, Jesus was led into the wilderness by the Holy Spirit to be tempted by the devil. Each time the enemy offers some temptation (in this case, power and rule over every kingdom of the world), Jesus responds with Scripture and God's truth. This time, the third in the sequence, Jesus orders the enemy away and he flees.

Here's a cool Bible-reading tip: Anytime something is repeated, pay attention. There's usually a reason.

+ WHY DO YOU THINK JESUS REPEATS THE SAME LINE FROM MATTHEW 4 TO PETER?

This is so cool, guys! All the way back in the beginning of His earthly ministry, Satan tried to offer Jesus victory over the world without paying the price. He offered Jesus a shortcut. *I can give you what you want and you won't even have to die! All you have to do is worship me.* But Jesus was not falling for the trap. He knew that God's plan was greater and that He must follow it.

BEAUTIFUL KINGDOM

Then, later, His friend Peter tried to offer the same thing. *You won't have to die*, Peter said. *Never!* Jesus was prepared for this temptation. He knew what God had asked Him to do, and He was not about to allow His enemy to work through Peter to throw Him off track.

Of course His reaction was hard core! Peter was literally trying to tell Him not to die on the cross for us. That was His whole mission on earth! Peter needed Jesus's correction to get back on the right course, to realign His thoughts and heart with God's.

Often, we need the same thing.

We have to face it: Correction is going to happen. We are going to do things, think things, or feel things that don't line up with God's glorious plan, and we are going to need redirection. This is a *perk* of the beautiful Kingdom, not a constraint or a weight!

A broken thought pattern we see so often (one I have been guilty of more frequently than I'd like to admit) is the idea that the way we live or act doesn't matter because our eternity is already secured. *Why do I need to obey if I'm already saved? What does it matter?* But I think that stems from an incorrect understanding of what God's correction is! He doesn't just correct us because He's bored or because He needs us to follow a certain rule book so we can stay in His good graces. His correction is for our *protection*. It's a work of His great love for His children, intended to put us on the path of life! To gently guide us back to His light when we wander off into the dark.

Think about that conversation I had with my mentor. She knew that God had told me no to that opportunity as protection because He knew that it was going to lead me away from Him. His correction in my life and Her discernment to see it brought me freedom and helped me thrive and live my life to the fullest. I'm sure you can also think back on your life and see so many times where you may have been wrong and, once redirected, things

06 / WHEN JESUS CALLS YOU OUT

seemed to fall into place. Gosh, I don't know about you, but the older I get the more I become *grateful* and *desperate* for correction because I know that I need it.

Let's get super practical here! What does correction look like in our lives as college women? How does God deliver it to us? The most frequent and straightforward way that God redirects us is through His Word. Often, when we read our Bibles, we find out things about God that we don't imitate in our own lives. That spurs us to bend, to change to look a little more like the Father we love so much. Really, that's the most fool-proof way to experience God's guidance and, if you're new to hearing from the Lord, that's where I'd recommend you start.

But there are more ways God can correct us! Another is through the Holy Spirit. He will plant a feeling in your heart called "conviction." It's a holy kind of unrest that leads you to seek the Lord and turn your face to Him. This can happen right in the moment as you do or think something out of God's design, or it can come up in your spirit through prayer, worship, or time spent in His presence.

The third way we experience God's correction is through trusted Christians around us. I know that my mentor seeks God's heart and is consistently in His Word. I trusted her to deliver that correction to me because I trusted that God would speak through her. Perhaps you have some people in your life like that. Maybe it's a mentor, a pastor, your mom, your grandma, or even a heart-friend. But I do have to say, this method requires an abundance of caution and discernment. Ladies, we can't just let anyone and everyone speak into our lives! Seek God's heart and hold every word from another person up to the light of His understanding.

Now, if I were in your shoes, reading this chapter, I think I might feel the temptation to take it upon myself to be that "corrector" for all my friends. *They need me*, I'd think. *I should be correcting my friends more!* But I want to warn you . . . That's not what this is about. Sure, God will use us to speak into people's lives from time to time, but if you find that you are correcting others consistently but never receiving correction yourself, it might be time for a heart-check.

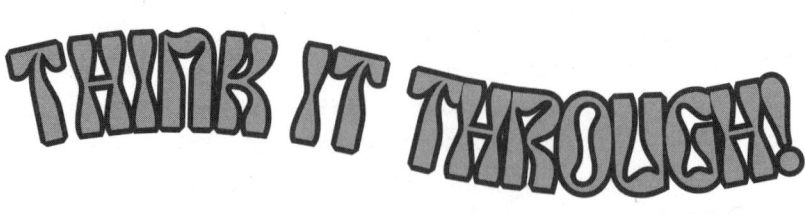

THINK IT THROUGH!

+ CAN YOU THINK OF A TIME WHEN GOD CORRECTED YOU? HOW DID HE DO IT? WHAT WAS IT LIKE?

+ WE LEARNED THREE WAYS TO EXPERIENCE GOD'S CORRECTION (HIS WORD, HOLY SPIRIT CONVICTION, AND TRUSTED ADVICE). WHICH IS MOST COMFORTABLE FOR YOU? WHICH DO YOU WANT TO GROW IN?

06 / WHEN JESUS CALLS YOU OUT

Let's jump back into the Scripture and wrap things up! Read Matthew 16:24–28.

3. HOLY HUMILITY

We've recognized our pride, we've opened ourselves up to correction, so what's the last step? We step into holy humility!

I love this piece of Scripture because it's so reminiscent of the upside-down, unexpected Kingdom that Jesus is announcing. On the surface, it makes no sense. How do we gain our life by losing it? How do we save our lives but lose our souls? But when we look at Jesus (our very favorite place to look), we see the perfect example of holy humility.

Jesus lost His life so we could find eternal life.

Jesus turned down an offer of the whole world, an easy reign, in favor of soul-rescue for His children.

Jesus, King of the universe, willingly went to the cross—a death He didn't deserve.

I don't know about you, but I want to be humble like Jesus! I want His correction and direction to wash over me, to clear out the pride I've allowed to take root, and to remake me into something beautiful. An image-bearer of the King.

If we skip forward in Matthew a little bit, we'll find more of Jesus's heart for humility. And that's where we'll end for this week.

Read Matthew 18:1–5.

> **"THEREFORE, WHOEVER TAKES THE LOWLY POSITION OF THIS CHILD IS THE GREATEST IN THE KINGDOM OF HEAVEN."**
> **Matthew 18:4**

BEAUTIFUL KINGDOM

Jesus asks us to be like children. To lose our pride—the lives we've built up for ourselves, standing on our own power—and to gain His new life. A child knows they have more to learn. A child relies totally on their dad for survival. A child expects correction; without it, how would they grow? A child runs in for a hug without hesitation. A child is *needy*, not self-reliant.

So where does that leave us? We've acknowledged that we have pride, selfish sin patterns that try to wreck us and sneak in when we least expect it. We know we're called to bring it the light, to hold every aspect of our lives up for inspection by a gentle Savior. We've opened ourselves up to correction, embraced it. And now, do you feel new?

You can start fresh right now. You can be a little child in the arms of your Father, connected to Him in dependence, ready to follow where He leads. You are a humble friend of the Most High King.

STOP AND PRAY!

THANK YOU, GOD, FOR CALLING US OUT. WE LOVE IT WHEN YOU MAKE US NEW.

06 / WHEN JESUS CALLS YOU OUT

BEAUTIFUL KINGDOM

CONVERSATION STARTERS

1. Be honest... What was your initial reaction to this Scripture? Are you familiar with it? Was it confusing, uncomfortable, convicting? Process your thoughts below.

2. Did you feel the Lord convict you of any area of pride in your life while reading this chapter? What was it?

06 / WHEN JESUS CALLS YOU OUT

3. Think back on a time when you received correction from the Lord, whether by reading His Word, Holy Spirit conviction, or from a trusted friend. How did you respond? How did it unlock growth in your life or in your relationship with the Lord?

4. This Scripture empowers us to start fresh, to be children in the arms of our Father. What do you feel empowered to step into this week?

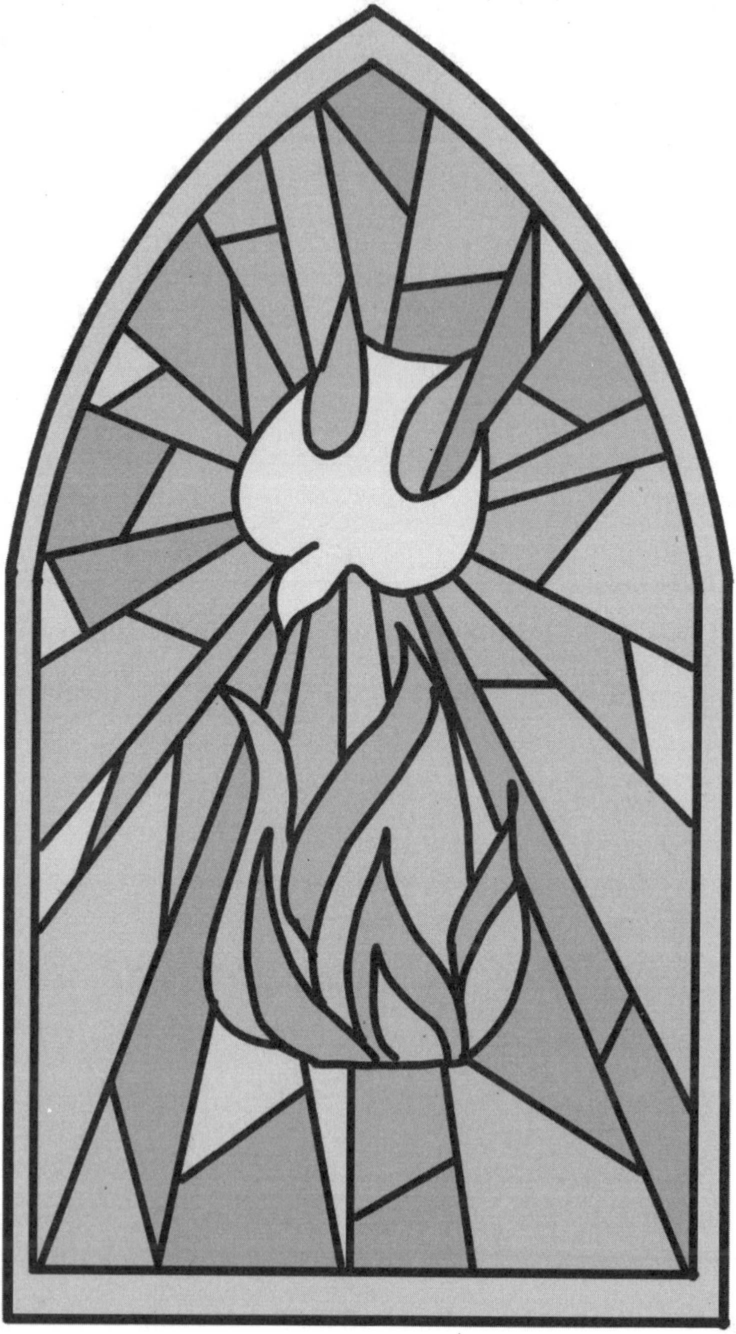

GLORY

CHAPTER 7

BEAUTIFUL KINGDOM

GLORY

Matthew 17:1 – 8

Imagine this. Your best friend invites you and a couple buddies to hike to the top of a mountain. When you get to the top, your friend suddenly starts glowing—yes, *glowing*—then two famous dead guys appear right next to him. Then, on top of all that, a loud voice from the sky joins the conversation. Right as you're about to keel over from terror, it all goes away and you're left standing next to your friends again.

Objectively, that's absolutely *wild*. I mean, has anything like that ever happened to you? No way! But that mountain trip—known as the Transfiguration—is part of the history of Jesus, as weird or crazy as it sounds. It's here, in the book of Matthew, ready for us to read and try to understand. It was a holy moment so important that it made it into the Bible! Hard to comprehend? Maybe. But crucial to our understanding of our Savior? Definitely.

OK, God, You have our attention! You can find this story in Matthew 17:1–8. Go ahead and check it out before we go any further.

I think sometimes we allow Jesus to become normal. We start to think of Him casually, finding ourselves a little too comfortable

07 / GLORY

with our understanding of Him. Supernatural can start to feel natural; awe-inspiring can start to feel everyday. But it's stories like this that shock our systems back into alignment, that renew our minds to see the beauty of Jesus as He is. Not watered down so He's easier to consume, not shrunken to our size, and not normalized for comfort.

We've spent seven weeks studying the book of Matthew for glimpses of the beautiful Kingdom Jesus came to announce. But we can't forget that His Kingdom doesn't look like what we're used to. We can't forget that Jesus is bigger than we thought He was. In our reading this week, I believe that God is inviting us to see Jesus as He really is: majestic and glorious, deserving of our awe and wonder.

So let's dive into the story of the Transfiguration and see what God has in store!

STOP AND PRAY!

LORD, GIVE ME A FRESH AWE AND WONDER FOR YOUR GLORY AND YOUR MAJESTY. I WANT TO SEE YOUR BEAUTY!

BEAUTIFUL KINGDOM

+ FILL IN THE BLANKS FROM MATTHEW 17:1–3.

"AFTER SIX DAYS JESUS TOOK WITH HIM _____, _____ AND _____ THE BROTHER OF JAMES, AND LED THEM UP A HIGH MOUNTAIN BY THEMSELVES. THERE HE WAS _____ BEFORE THEM. HIS FACE SHONE LIKE THE SUN, AND HIS CLOTHES BECAME AS WHITE AS THE LIGHT. JUST THEN THERE APPEARED BEFORE THEM MOSES AND ELIJAH, TALKING WITH JESUS."
MATTHEW 17:1–3

About a week after Peter's prideful moment we discussed in the last chapter, Jesus invited three of His closest disciples (Peter, James, and John) to come up a mountain with Him. And what happened there was so significant that both Peter and John recounted it later on in their own writings (John 1:14, 2 Peter 1:16) and it was mentioned in three out of four Gospels. This moment is what's known as "the Transfiguration."

> **FUN FACT!**
> "Transfigure" isn't a term we hear a lot in our modern-day vernacular. Written as *metamorphoo* in the original Greek, it's a word that means to change or transform.

Admittedly, this story can feel like a lot to take in all at once, so let's just take it piece by piece. Look back at those three verses above (Matthew 17:1–3). There's enough in just those three verses for us to chew on for years, so we'll narrow it down a little. What's the first thing we notice as we read the beginning of this story? The glory and majesty of Jesus.

07 / GLORY

1. JESUS IS GLORIOUS.

Sometime last year, I walked out of my apartment with some friends, all on our way to hop in our cars and drive to dinner. It was early evening, right in that moment when it's not too light but not too dark out. And as we headed to our cars, we all stopped short, one by one. It was like a movie scene! Perfectly choreographed jaw drops and wide eyes.

Can you guess what stopped us short? The sunset was *breathtaking*, one of the most beautiful I'd ever seen. The whole sky was a soft, dusky pink. There were clouds scattered throughout, seeming like giant pieces of pink cotton candy floating around. And the sun, almost all the way down for the evening, was glowing in a way that inspired so much awe for us that all we could do was stare.

It's moments like that one that make me think of glory. When I see a beautiful sunset, hand-painted by God, I'm reminded of His beauty, His majesty.

Do you think the disciples had that sunset moment when Jesus was transfigured before them? The Scripture says that *His face shone like the sun*. They must have been just as enamored by the beauty as we are when we see a sunset. Imagine! This man they had lived with for years and had begun to realize was something more—God in their midst—suddenly looked like an angel. He'd been telling them over and over about the Kingdom of Heaven, but then they got to witness it right in front of their eyes.

And as out-of-pocket as this moment seems for our modern context (I'm sure so many of us are wondering why Jesus was glowing right now!), it actually wasn't too far out of the disciples' realm of understanding. In fact, there was precedent for a moment like this in the Hebrew Scriptures.

BEAUTIFUL KINGDOM

+ READ EXODUS 33:18–23. SUMMARIZE WHAT HAPPENED IN THE SPACE BELOW.

Moses, over a thousand years before Jesus came on the scene, asked for a glimpse of God's glory. And the whole moment was kind of dangerous! Reading it sounds like reading a warning label. *Keep your eyes closed! Don't get too close!* But check out what happened just a few verses later when Moses came down from the mountain of God's glory.

> "WHEN MOSES CAME DOWN FROM MOUNT SINAI WITH THE TWO TABLETS OF THE COVENANT LAW IN HIS HANDS, HE WAS NOT AWARE THAT <u>HIS FACE WAS RADIANT BECAUSE HE HAD SPOKEN WITH THE LORD</u>. WHEN AARON AND ALL THE ISRAELITES SAW MOSES, HIS FACE WAS RADIANT, AND THEY WERE AFRAID TO COME NEAR HIM."
> Exodus 34:29–30, emphasis added

Because Moses had spent time in the presence of a holy God, His face was *radiant* (literally the Hebrew word there means shiny!). Sound familiar? On the mount of transfiguration, the disciples got a glimpse of the glory of God reflected in Jesus. It was like He peeled back Heaven's curtains and let Peter, James, and John peek in.

07 / GLORY

And the crazy thing is as we read in the very next verse, Moses was actually there! Alongside Elijah—an Old Testament prophet—Moses and Jesus were having a casual conversation. Understandably, the disciples were freaking out. Moses and Elijah appearing there must have been more confirmation for the disciples that Jesus really was the Messiah, the completion and fulfillment of the entire Old Testament, the Scriptures they had grown up memorizing. They were, without a doubt, in the presence of God.

When have you felt the presence of God? Maybe you felt Him at a worship night as you sang along to songs of praise. Maybe you felt His presence in a hard moment when you sought Him in desperate prayer. Maybe you felt His presence when faced with something beautiful, like that sunset. It's that awe-inspiring and humbling feeling of being part of something much greater than yourself.

But so often, we don't see the glory of God. We go to a worship night with closed-off hearts, just there to keep up appearances and go through the motions. We find ourselves praying out of habit, talking to Jesus like an acquaintance we have a few minutes to catch up with between classes. We even find ourselves walking right past a beautiful sunset with no wonder stirring in our hearts. Could it be that we've forgotten about the glory of God? Could it be that we've, not even intentionally, normalized the movements of Jesus? Have we shrunk Him to fit our understanding?

I don't know about you, but I want my eyes wide open to witness God's glory.

+ CAN YOU THINK OF A TIME WHEN YOU FELT THE PRESENCE OF GOD? WHAT WAS IT LIKE?

BEAUTIFUL KINGDOM

Let's keep moving! Take a look at the next two verses.

> "PETER SAID TO JESUS, 'LORD, IT IS GOOD FOR US TO BE HERE. IF YOU WISH, I WILL PUT UP THREE SHELTERS—ONE FOR YOU, ONE FOR MOSES AND ONE FOR ELIJAH.' WHILE HE WAS STILL SPEAKING, A BRIGHT CLOUD COVERED THEM, AND A VOICE FROM THE CLOUD SAID, 'THIS IS MY SON, WHOM I LOVE; WITH HIM I AM WELL PLEASED. LISTEN TO HIM!'"
> **Matthew 17:4–5**

If we learned anything about Peter from last week, it's that he's relatable. I love this moment! With the extra context we're given in Mark and Luke, we learn that Peter was actually so shocked and overwhelmed by what was going on that he just blurted that sentence out.

TAKE IT DEEPER...
The presence and glory of God often shows up in the Bible as a bright cloud. Check out Exodus 13:22; 16:10; 19:9; and Numbers 12:5.

Uh, this is good! Let's hang out here forever!

Scholars interpret Peter's reaction in lots of different ways, but I like to think that He was experiencing the presence of God and knew, deep in his soul, that it's *good* to be there, weird shelter talk aside. So many of us have felt that way before! God has hardwired this special desire within us to crave His glorious presence.

Now, speaking of glory, let's take a closer look at what God had to say from the cloud.

07 / GLORY

2. DELIGHT IN JESUS.

Do you remember the moment in Matthew 3 we learned about all the way back in chapter one? During Jesus's baptism, when the Heavens opened and God spoke, what did He say?

+ FIND MATTHEW 3:17 IN YOUR BIBLE AND COPY DOWN WHAT GOD SAID IN THE SPACE BELOW.

It sounds familiar, right!? Every time something is repeated in Scripture, it means it's important and that we need to pay attention. And what did God choose to repeat? *His love for Jesus!*

The heart of the Father is to love His son. We've seen it time and time again in our study of Scripture. God's most prevailing character trait is love, especially love for His only son, Jesus. Here again, God is reminding Peter, James, and John—and by extension, us—of that love. In some translations, it says that God *delights* in Jesus.

And the Bible also says that God delights in us!

+ FILL IN THE BLANKS FROM PSALM 147:11.

"THE Lord _____ IN THOSE WHO FEAR HIM, WHO PUT THEIR HOPE IN HIS UNFAILING _____."

BEAUTIFUL KINGDOM

So here's the question . . . Do you love Jesus like God does? Do you delight in your Savior? Because He delights in you! He numbered every hair on your head, He's a witness to every thought in your mind, and He catches each one of your tears. He made that beautiful sunrise and that latte you love so much, that majestic ocean view and that cute new journal you bought last week. He shadows your every step, patiently guiding you into paths of His presence. Doesn't that make you want to delight right back?

It's the natural next step to realigning your heart to awe and wonder of the glory of God. When you see Him rightly, when you're a witness to His majesty, it only makes sense that your love for Him would grow. Just like Peter overwhelmingly craved more time in His presence, when we behold His glory, our hearts are moved toward delight.

I know this sounds a little up-in-the-clouds, but hang with me here! It's actually super simple to apply to our everyday lives. *Do you delight in Jesus?* This can look like worship that's filled with praise, a celebration of the beauty of our Savior. It can look like adoration throughout the day, choosing attributes of God to meditate on. It can look like calling out His glory as you see it, going through life with eyes wide open to His wonder.

Jesus, we want to delight in You! You are so worthy of our love!

LET'S PRACTICE DELIGHT!

+ READ PSALM 139:14 AND COPY IT DOWN IN THE SPACE ON THE NEXT PAGE.

07 / GLORY

[ ]

+ WHICH OF HIS "WONDERFUL WORKS" COMES TO MIND AS YOU READ THAT VERSE? MAYBE IT'S SOMETHING GOOD HE'S DONE IN YOUR LIFE, SOMETHING BEAUTIFUL YOU'VE WITNESSED RECENTLY, OR A STORY FROM THE BIBLE YOU LOVE.

[ ]

+ NOW, DELIGHT IN HIM! WRITE OUT YOUR PRAYERS BELOW. PRAISE HIM FOR THAT WONDROUS WORK. TELL HIM HOW MUCH YOU LOVE HIM!

[ ]

God is doing something profound in our hearts through the story of the Transfiguration. Can you feel it? He's tenderly realigning our vision, helping us to see Him rightly, and wooing our hearts to His. So let's wrap this story up and see where He wants to lead us next.

> "WHEN THE DISCIPLES HEARD THIS, THEY FELL FACEDOWN TO THE GROUND, TERRIFIED. BUT JESUS CAME AND TOUCHED THEM. 'GET UP,' HE SAID. 'DON'T BE AFRAID.' WHEN THEY LOOKED UP, THEY SAW NO ONE EXCEPT JESUS."
> Matthew 17:6–8

3. DON'T BE AFRAID.

What do you think of when you hear "fear of God"? Maybe it brings a negative connotation up for you, memories of fear tactics used on you as a kid to get you to behave or hurt from a church that shamed you into submission. Maybe it makes you think of fear you have of your earthly father or maybe fear of letting God down or disappointing Him.

Whatever your past with this "fear" is, we can view the ending to this story as an invitation to be terrified *and* unafraid. You see, there is such a thing as a healthy fear of God; it's a good thing! When we open our eyes to His glory and when we turn our hearts toward Him, it brings with it a new kind of honor for His name. We aren't scared of Him, but we respect Him. We know that He is bigger than we are—different from us and unsearchable.

The disciples were instinctively reacting to that awe-inspiring holiness when they heard God's voice and fell face down on the ground, terrified. I'd venture a guess to say that all of us would have

07 / GLORY

reacted the same way. The wonder of His presence *should* bring us to our knees.

We love to get too comfortable with God. I've found myself time and time again referring to Him as my buddy, the big guy upstairs. And in part, He is our buddy; He sent Jesus to us so that He could call us friends! But He is still God. How often do we forget that? Our culture has strayed so far from holy fear and awe. Is it possible we're missing out on a whole side of His character by normalizing Him? By putting Him in a small, approachable, easy to digest box?

This story is a reminder that our God isn't ordinary and that we shouldn't let Him be. But even more earth shattering and mind bending is the very next line in the passage.

+ FILL IN THE BLANKS FROM MATTHEW 17:7.

"BUT JESUS CAME AND TOUCHED THEM. 'GET UP,' HE SAID. '_____ _____ _____.'"

Don't be afraid. Let that sink in for a second. What a beautiful image of Jesus! What a picture of the upside-down Kingdom of Heaven! He is inviting us to stand with Him, unafraid. He died on the cross so that we could approach Him with confidence, so that we could become coheirs of the Kingdom. Yes, we are in awe of Him. Yes, we respect Him. But also, we share in His glory. We get to bask in the radiance of His face, invited to become more like Him as we spend time in His presence.

What a moment! I can picture Jesus reaching out His hand and setting it on Peter's shoulder. *I know, it's a lot. But I'm here. You don't have to be scared.*

BEAUTIFUL KINGDOM

You are welcomed into the holy, wonderful, and glorious presence of an almighty God. You are invited to see Him rightly, to see His glory without a veil or a cover (2 Corinthians 3:18). You are invited to love Him like He loves you, to delight in His presence. And you are invited to live in unity with Him, aware of His bigness but content in His welcoming arms.

I want to encourage you to let this Scripture change your heart little by little. You don't have to close your book and turn your whole life upside down, filled with shame for the times you forgot how mighty God is and promising yourself to try harder to honor Him. That would be such a miss! Instead, let this be like a warm blanket, a soft wind that will fan into flame the embers of love and adoration we hold in our hearts for our Savior.

> **"WHEN THEY LOOKED UP, THEY SAW NO ONE EXCEPT JESUS."**
> **Matthew 17:8**

Our Jesus is beautiful! His Kingdom is beautiful! And every day, we get to love Him more.

07 / GLORY

BEAUTIFUL KINGDOM

CONVERSATION STARTERS

1. What aspect of God's character stood out to you from this week's Scripture? Was there anything that surprised you?

2. Is your natural tendency to see God more as big and scary or normal and comfortable? How do you think that affects the way you relate to Him?

07 / GLORY

3. What in your life makes you think of God's glory (a sunset, a moment of worship, etc.)? How does it make you feel?

4. What's one of the things you *love* about Jesus in this season of your life? What's one way you can delight in Him this week?

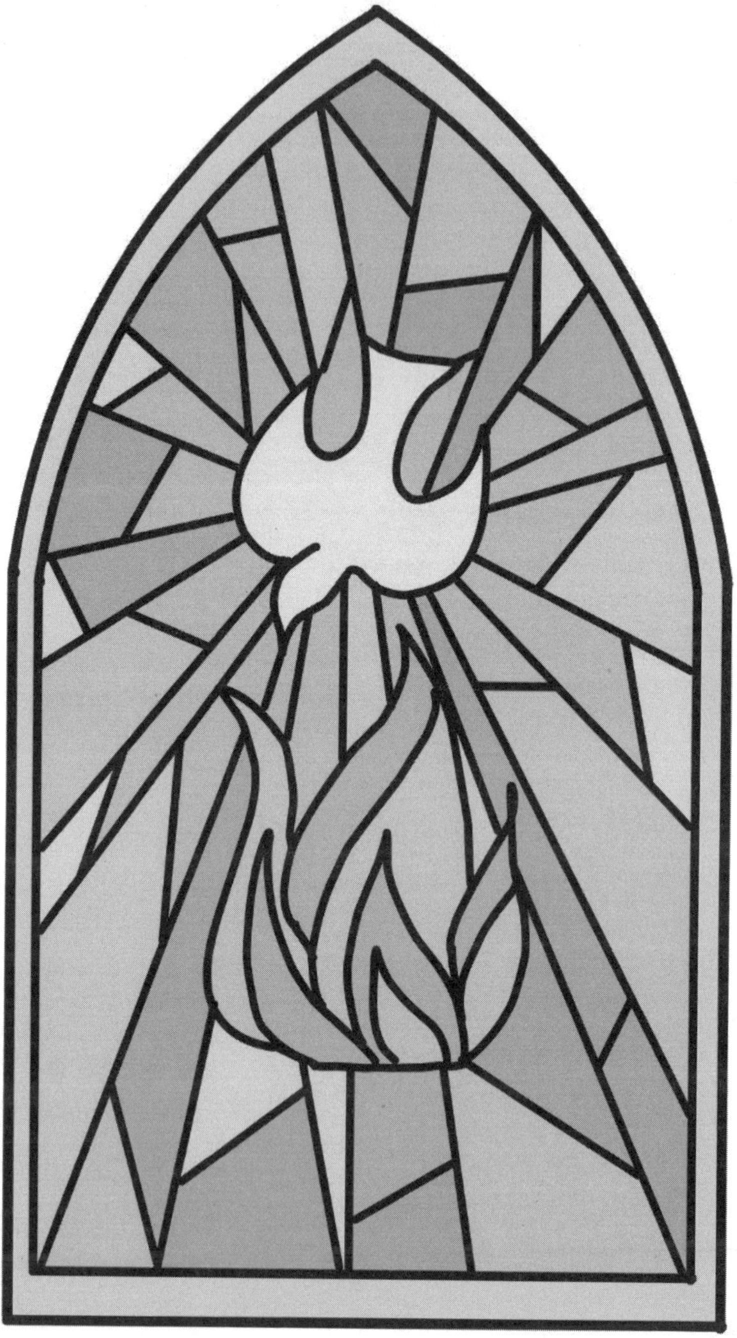

FOR THE LEAST OF THESE

CHAPTER 8

BEAUTIFUL KINGDOM

FOR THE LEAST OF THESE

Matthew 25 - 26

> "WHOEVER IS KIND TO THE POOR LENDS TO THE Lord, AND HE WILL REWARD THEM FOR WHAT THEY HAVE DONE."
> **Proverbs 19:17**

Generosity. It's a value close to our hearts as a ministry. You'll see it played out in Delight chapters across the nation as they serve their communities together. And if you've been around the Christian church for a while, you'll know that it's also a core part of who we

08 / FOR THE LEAST OF THESE

are: as Christians, we are generous with our time, our money, and our love. It's foundational—a basic, ground-level heart-posture we all strive to take.

Perhaps you've been encouraged to tithe to your local church, invited on an overseas mission trip, or tagged along with some friends to serve in a soup kitchen. In so many ways, I believe that we are surrounded by people who are cheerful givers, people who go above and beyond, sacrificing for strangers, all with a smile on their face. And that is commendable! What a joy it is to see a community all-in with Jesus go all-out in serving His children!

But do you ever feel like you give just to give and then forget why you do it? I don't know about you, but I've shown up to service events far more excited to hang out with my friends than to serve the people I'm there to help. I've written cards for hospital patients or veterans just so I could check it off my community service list. I've even given money to people on the street just to look like a good Christian for the people watching. We can get so caught up in doing the right thing that we lose track of why we're doing it in the first place—what it really means to unlock generosity in our hearts.

This week we're going to look through two chapters of the book of Matthew in search of Jesus's heart for generosity. Think of these moments like podcast sound bites you'd see on Instagram. They're little hints—captured glimpses—that give us a picture of the greater story. And the greater story here, the story Matthew is telling about Jesus's majestic and lowly announcement and inauguration of the Kingdom of Heaven, is running full speed ahead as we step into Matthew chapter 25.

We left off last week in chapter 17, where Jesus was transfigured in front of a few of His closest disciples. From there He went on to perform more healings, teach many parables, and even make His grand entrance into Jerusalem (one He knew would end in His death). If you were to take a quick read through these interim chapters, you'd notice a bit of a tone switch. Things seem to be getting more urgent; Jesus's teachings begin to sound a lot more like warnings, and He begins to talk about His coming death and even the "end times." It's there, in that end time discourse, that we find our first generosity soundbite.

I know what you're thinking... *There's a generosity message in a teaching about the end of the world? No way!* I know it sounds wild, but it's just further proof that giving to the needy and serving our community is important to Jesus. It's so important that He'd tie it into His warnings about the age to come.

Let's prepare our hearts and dive in!

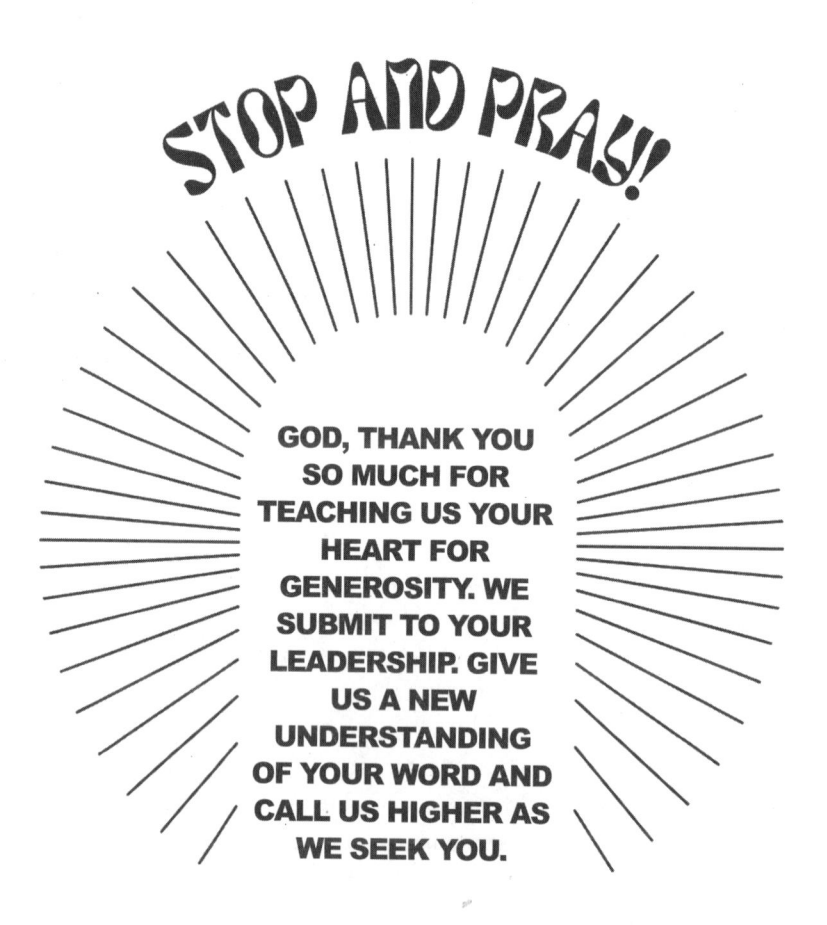

STOP AND PRAY!

GOD, THANK YOU SO MUCH FOR TEACHING US YOUR HEART FOR GENEROSITY. WE SUBMIT TO YOUR LEADERSHIP. GIVE US A NEW UNDERSTANDING OF YOUR WORD AND CALL US HIGHER AS WE SEEK YOU.

08 / FOR THE LEAST OF THESE

Read Matthew 25:31–46.

+ WHAT ARE YOUR INITIAL REACTIONS WHEN READING THIS PASSAGE?

Wow. That was a lot. If I'm being honest, reading that passage kind of makes me want to hide under my bed and never come out. I can only imagine how Jesus's original audience felt hearing it straight from His mouth. There is some pretty strong language in there—themes that can be scary and shocking. But I want to encourage you to lean in! This is not a conversation meant to scare you or condemn you. It's a beautiful reminder. A refresh and a reset.

Much smarter Bible readers than I have studied these words in depth and have come up with many conclusions about what, as a whole, Jesus was alluding to. I'm going to do my best to give us a broad overview of the context then help us zoom in to the underlying heart for generosity we find there.

First, some context! This moment in Matthew comes at the tail end of some very teaching-heavy chapters where Jesus's favorite method to get His point across was through *parables*. Parables are simple stories used to illustrate moral or spiritual lessons.[1] Some of the more famous ones include the parable of the sower, the parable of the good Samaritan, and the parable of the lost sheep. These are moments where Jesus employs His creativity to illustrate a point for us. They aren't retellings of real-life events (as far as we know) but are a way to help us understand what Jesus is teaching.

The Scripture we just read is kind of like a parable, but kind of not. It starts off sounding like one with all the sheep and goats talk, but then seems to lean more straightforward as it goes along. I like to think that it's Jesus's way of explaining the two parables He delivered in the beginning of Matthew 25—the parable of the ten virgins and the parable of the bags of gold—both of which talk about the same topic: how to be prepared for the end of days.

Now we're not getting into an end-times conversation this week. Though, we do highly encourage you to do your own research on this topic (Hint: the book of Revelation is a great place to start). Instead, hidden inside this pseudo-parable, we're going to look for Jesus's heart for generosity.

+ FILL IN THE BLANKS FROM MATTHEW 25:40.

"'TRULY I TELL YOU, WHATEVER YOU DID FOR ONE OF THE _____ OF THESE BROTHERS AND SISTERS OF MINE, YOU DID FOR ____.'"

It's there, loud and clear. The way we serve others is important to Jesus. And judging by the tone of the passage, it's *vitally* important.

1. WE ARE CALLED TO BE GENEROUS.

My husband feeds the hungry for a living. It's been his passion for as long as I've known him—spurred by a nonprofit his family started after reading these very verses we're discussing—and I am constantly in awe of his tireless generosity and compassion toward the people all around us who don't have enough food to eat. The weekend before I was set to write this chapter, he had a Saturday morning distribution scheduled, a drive-through food pickup for families in need.

08 / FOR THE LEAST OF THESE

Confession time: I really didn't want to go. In all honesty, I don't usually go with him when he serves. Call it laziness, selfishness, or a mixture of the two, but I am normally content to let him feed the hungry while I get a few extra hours of sleep. But this weekend, I felt God nudge my heart. *You should go*, I felt Him say. *Experience this Scripture for yourself.*

That was just the nudge I needed to get myself in gear and join my husband to distribute food. And let me tell you, it was so amazing! Not only did we have a blast meeting members of our community, but we got to see God's love in action for people who were desperately in need. And I learned a valuable lesson: we're not called to sit on the sideline.

It's like what Jesus was describing:

> **"FOR I WAS HUNGRY AND YOU GAVE ME SOMETHING TO EAT, I WAS THIRSTY AND YOU GAVE ME SOMETHING TO DRINK, I WAS A STRANGER AND YOU INVITED ME IN, I NEEDED CLOTHES AND YOU CLOTHED ME, I WAS SICK AND YOU LOOKED AFTER ME, I WAS IN PRISON AND YOU CAME TO VISIT ME.'"**
> **Matthew 25:35–36**

+ LOOK BACK AT THAT VERSE AND CIRCLE EVERY TIME IT SAYS "YOU."

I wonder if part of our complacency toward service and generosity is because we are content to let other people do it for us. We aren't villains, choosing not to serve our community because we want to see them suffer. I think that most of us reading this really do want to love our neighbor! But we find ourselves stuck in a hands-off kind of mindset. We skip the events because we just don't have the time in our schedule, promising to drop a dollar in the donation jar at the next opportunity. We find ourselves at a soup kitchen with our Delight chapter wondering why it's been so long since we've done something like this. We drive past someone in need and hope that somebody else stops to help.

But look back at the Scripture! Jesus makes it so clear that our generosity is supposed to be personal, a calling on our lives we are meant to take seriously, not neglect out of apathy or disinterest. *You* gave him something to eat, not *they*. If we really buy into the idea that when we serve the most vulnerable we're really serving Jesus our Savior, then we have to buy into the warning that comes attached to it.

> **"TRULY I TELL YOU, WHATEVER YOU DID NOT DO FOR ONE OF THE LEAST OF THESE, YOU DID NOT DO FOR ME."**
> Matthew 25:45, emphasis added

Now, this is not meant as a scare tactic. I know these verses can be intimidating to read! But they are meant to be motivators just as much as warnings. It's like flipping a light switch in our brains, jogging our memories and getting our feet moving to serve the people Jesus died for. We have to know this: you can't serve your way into Heaven. Only faith in Jesus can do that! But, your generosity is an outward sign of the work God is doing in your heart. It's a fruit you are called and inspired to bear when you are living a life that's connected to Him.

When we let this warning soak in, it simply breaks our heart for what breaks Jesus's heart. Reminded and rejuvenated, we become eager to accept this calling and go all in.

08 / FOR THE LEAST OF THESE

+ CAN YOU THINK OF A TIME WHERE YOU SERVED YOUR COMMUNITY? WHAT WAS IT LIKE?

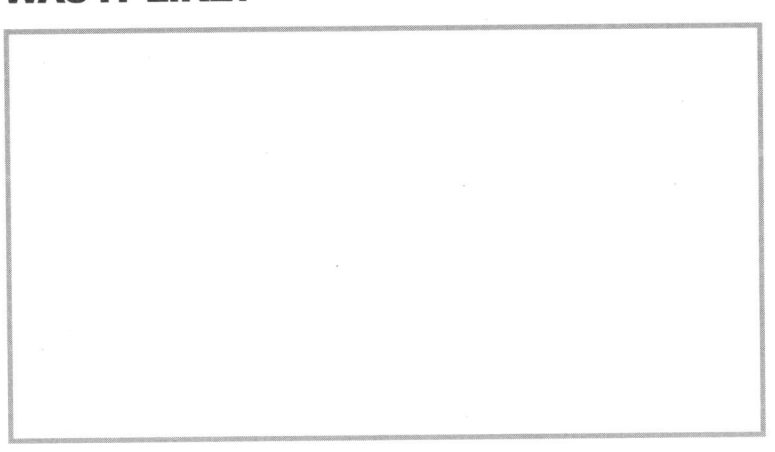

Let's move on to our next sound bite! Flip in your Bible to Matthew 26 and read verses 6–13.

I don't know about you, but I have always loved this moment in Scripture! I'm captivated by the woman's devotion to Jesus as she pours her worship out for Him. Maybe you've studied this moment before and felt called to be more like Mary (we learn her name from the other gospel accounts) and to be unafraid of everyone's opinions as you worship Jesus. Or maybe you were struck by her extravagance and wanted to give Jesus your very best.

FUN FACT!
A variation of this moment shows up in all four Gospels! Something about Mary's extravagant worship captured the attention of each Gospel author. How beautiful is that!?

But have you ever read it and noticed the generosity conversation woven in?

The disciples weren't too happy about it when Mary poured the expensive perfume out for Jesus.

BEAUTIFUL KINGDOM

> "WHEN THE DISCIPLES SAW THIS, THEY WERE INDIGNANT. 'WHY THIS WASTE?' THEY ASKED. 'THIS PERFUME COULD HAVE BEEN SOLD AT A HIGH PRICE AND THE MONEY GIVEN TO THE POOR.'"
> Matthew 26:8-9

And if you think about it, this reaction makes sense. They had just heard Jesus preach about the importance of giving to the poor. They'd clearly taken His warning seriously (though we learn that one disciple, Judas, just wanted to keep the money for himself). I wonder if they thought Jesus would be proud of them for calling her out. Maybe they thought they'd get extra brownie points for remembering the poor.

But how did Jesus respond?

+ FILL IN THE BLANKS FROM MATTHEW 26:10–11.

"AWARE OF THIS, JESUS SAID TO THEM, 'WHY ARE YOU BOTHERING THIS WOMAN? SHE HAS DONE A BEAUTIFUL THING TO ME. THE _____ YOU WILL ALWAYS HAVE WITH YOU, BUT YOU WILL NOT ALWAYS HAVE ____."

What's going on here? Is Jesus contradicting the hard-core warning He just gave about giving to the poor? No way. He's actually *deepening* it. Here, Jesus is addressing our hearts.

2. YOUR HEART MATTERS.

08 / FOR THE LEAST OF THESE

Look back at the difference between Mary's posture and the disciples'. She was giving extravagantly, generosity flowing from her every pore. That perfume could have been all she had, certainly a costly offering. She poured it on Jesus's head as an act of worship. She was so focused on Him that she didn't care what everyone else was thinking; she just gave because she loved Him.

The disciples stood there and watched, uncomfortable with her extravagance. They thought it was wasteful. Why pour it all on Jesus when it could have been sold and given away? Isn't that what Jesus said to do?

So often, we listen to what Jesus says, making mental lists of to-dos as we read our Bibles, but we completely miss the heart of the One who's speaking. The disciples heard "give," and they counted the cost, trying to do the right thing but missing the point. Mary heard "give" and let the love she had for her Savior and friend guide her. She poured it all out just for Him.

And Jesus said her act of generosity was *beautiful*.

Do you think that's where we need to start? Before we scramble off our couches and start a new nonprofit or donate all of our money to a local homeless shelter, we need to first allow the love we have for our Savior to move us to extravagant worship. We pour it all out at His feet first, giving Him our everything because we know that's what He deserves. And then, out of the overflow, He will call us to give to the needy, directing our love for Him to the people He loves.

This is an honor! We get to come to Jesus like Mary. He is worth every ounce of love, affection, and worship we have to give. That is the home base where we learn how to properly give to others. When we have our eyes focused on Him, serving our community—which we are definitely called to do—begins to feel less like an obligation and more like an outpouring of fragrant perfume for our God.

BEAUTIFUL KINGDOM

Remember what Jesus said!

> **"TRULY I TELL YOU, WHATEVER YOU DID FOR ONE OF THE LEAST OF THESE BROTHERS AND SISTERS OF MINE, YOU DID FOR ME."**
> Matthew 25:40, emphasis added

Our heart is that you would read these moments in Scripture and feel excited to serve and give and love the people around you. But it's so crucial that we do it out of the right heart. We don't just want empty obedience! We want all-in women of God who love Jesus so much that the deepest desire of their hearts is to follow where He leads and to love who He loves. It's a subtle change, but it's one that could transform your life.

THINK IT THROUGH!

+ WHEN READING THIS STORY, WHICH REACTION REFLECTS YOU MORE IN THIS SEASON? ARE YOU MORE LIKE MARY, POURING EVERYTHING OUT FOR JESUS OUT OF LOVE, OR ARE YOU MORE LIKE THE DISCIPLES, STRIVING TO BE OBEDIENT BUT COUNTING THE COST? PROCESS ON THE NEXT PAGE!

08 / FOR THE LEAST OF THESE

+ CAN YOU THINK OF A TIME WHERE YOU SERVED OR GAVE WITH THE WRONG HEART-POSTURE? HOW MIGHT IT LOOK DIFFERENT WITH YOUR HEART FOCUSED ON EXTRAVAGANT LOVE FOR JESUS?

Let's move on to sound bite number three. I have to say, this one might be my favorite!

Read Matthew 26:26–30.

BEAUTIFUL KINGDOM

+ HAVE YOU READ THIS PASSAGE BEFORE? WHAT IS YOUR UNDERSTANDING OF THE LAST SUPPER AND COMMUNION?

This is another one of those uber-famous passages, and for good reason. Here, Jesus is reclining at the table just hours before His death and sharing one last meal with the disciples during Passover, a Jewish festival celebrating God's protection over the Israelites when they were enslaved in Egypt. He had just finished telling the disciples (His closest friends) that one of them was going to betray Him. The tone was heavy and thick with unspoken questions, certainly a good amount of fear, and a tangible sorrow. And right in the midst of it all, Jesus held up a piece of bread and broke it.

> "WHILE THEY WERE EATING, JESUS TOOK BREAD, AND WHEN HE HAD GIVEN THANKS, HE BROKE IT AND GAVE IT TO HIS DISCIPLES, SAYING, 'TAKE AND EAT; THIS IS MY BODY.' THEN HE TOOK A CUP, AND WHEN HE HAD GIVEN THANKS, HE GAVE IT TO THEM, SAYING, 'DRINK FROM IT, ALL OF YOU. THIS IS MY BLOOD OF THE COVENANT, WHICH IS POURED OUT FOR MANY FOR THE FORGIVENESS OF SINS.'"
> Matthew 26:26–28

08 / FOR THE LEAST OF THESE

Take my body. I'm giving it to you. Take my blood. I'm pouring it out for you.

Do you see it? Nobody has ever given more than Jesus.

3. JESUS GAVE FIRST.

When we think of generosity, we have to think of sacrifice. When we donate a tenth of our income to our local church, it takes a certain acceptance that the money we earned doesn't get to stay in our bank account. *Sacrifice.* When we sign up to serve at a food drive on a Saturday morning, we know we have to get out of bed when we could have been sleeping. *Sacrifice.* When we agree to babysit free of charge because we know the parents are in a tough spot, it comes with an acknowledgement of money not earned. *Sacrifice.*

But it's so hard to get good at sacrifice. There's something hardwired in our broken nature that wants to hold on to our comfort—something inside of us that craves security. Sacrifice can be hard! But can you think of those times when it's easiest? I will drop everything to help my sister out when she gets a flat tire because I love her. I will buy my husband the most extravagant, expensive Christmas presents because I love him. I will go to bat for my best friends no matter the repercussions because I love them.

Love motivates sacrifice.

Did you know that Jesus loved you so much that He died for you? He walked straight toward torture and humiliation He didn't deserve *because He loved you.* He gave up everything *because He loved you.* He made the ultimate sacrifice *because He loved you.*

That's what He's talking about when He says that His body will be broken and His blood will be poured out for us! He used the bread and the wine as a way to illustrate for us just how far He was willing to go for our rescue. He gave his body, He gave His blood, for you and me!

BEAUTIFUL KINGDOM

That right there is the ultimate example of generosity. Jesus Christ is the best model of extravagant love. Isn't that just the image of the beautiful Kingodm? You can't ever outgive Jesus! He set a beautiful standard, one that He teaches us how to emulate little by little. Our extravagance is motivated by His extravagance! When we really and truly embrace the fact that He gave it all—that He gave the ultimate sacrifice—then generosity starts to flow out of us unhindered. He gave so much! Of course we can give what little we have!

I once found myself talking about generosity with a guy who worked in a phone store. I was telling Him about all the work my husband did to feed the hungry, and this man was shocked. He shared that he had grown up hungry and didn't know there were people out there who were willing to help. "I just don't see how you can have that kind of compassion," he said.

You know what we told him? "Well, Jesus had even bigger compassion for us. Why wouldn't we want to do the same for others?"

You are called to generosity. You are called to serve the poor and the needy and the helpless in your community. It's a Biblical mandate, a non-negotiable in the family of God. But the more you pour your worship out on Jesus, the more you meditate on the way that He poured His very body and blood out for you, the easier it becomes to sacrifice for those people. Your service and generosity should be and can be motivated by a pure heart for Jesus. Have you stepped into that? Have you allowed your King to change your heart-posture? He wants to unlock a holy compassion in your heart today. He wants you to be so overcome with love for Him that you can't help but show it to everyone you meet.

We can't outgive Jesus. But that's the beauty of it! He gave first so we can give now. Do you feel that fire rekindling in your heart? I can't wait to see the holy wave of extravagant givers He is about to unleash. Thank you, Lord!

08 / **FOR THE LEAST OF THESE**

BEAUTIFUL KINGDOM

CONVERSATION STARTERS

1. Which of the three points (We are called to be generous, Your heart matters, Jesus gave first) stood out to you the most? Why?

2. We love Mary's heart-posture of extravagant worship for Jesus. In what ways have you seen that same heart-posture at work in your life or in the lives of the people around you?

08 / FOR THE LEAST OF THESE

3. Jesus gave the ultimate sacrifice for us on the cross. What do you think holds us back from sacrificing for the people around us?

4. What's one tangible way you can practice generosity this week?

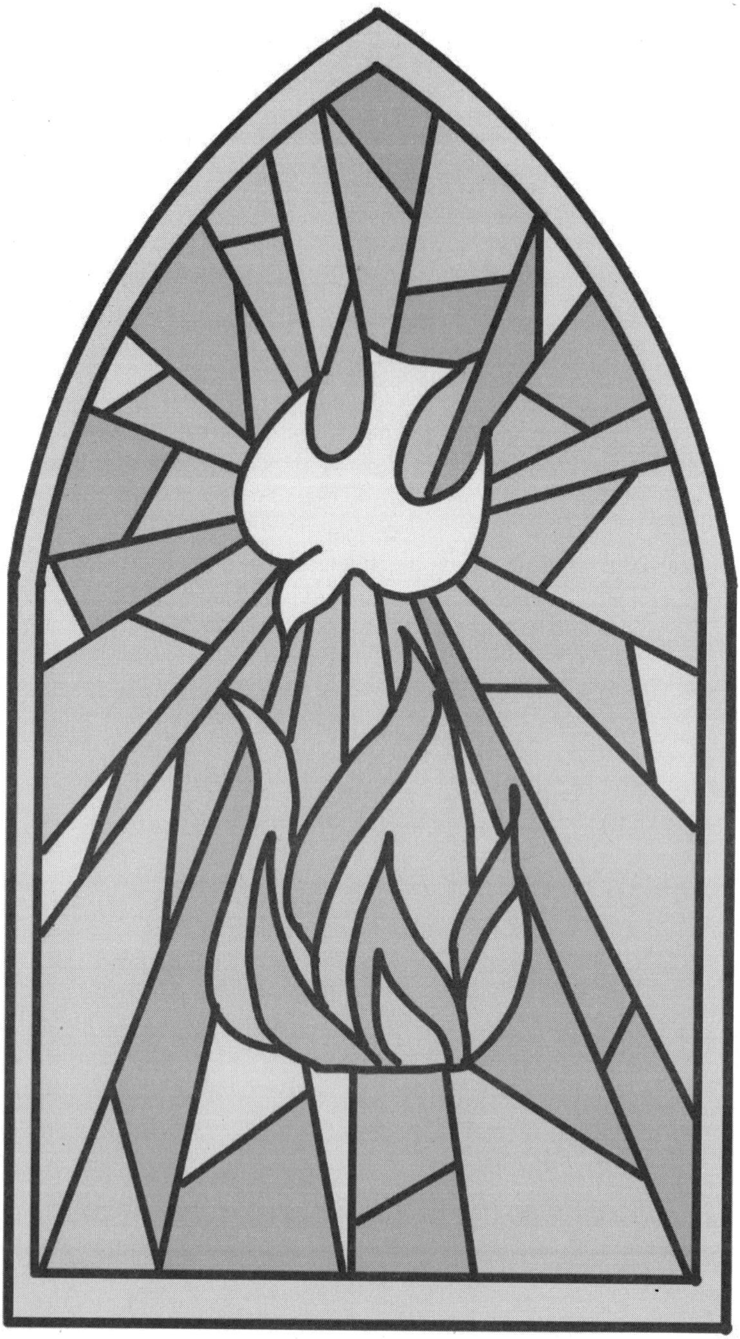

BEAUTIFUL TRUST

CHAPTER 9

BEAUTIFUL KINGDOM

BEAUTIFUL TRUST

Matthew 26 - 27

TRUST: Reliance on or confidence in a person.

GOD: Trustworthy (Proverbs 3:5–6, Psalm 20:7).

US: Trust issues.

09 / BEAUTIFUL TRUST

I won't go on roller coasters because I don't trust the tracks to hold up or the seat belt to keep me safe. I won't let my sister borrow my clothes because I don't trust that she'll give them back. I won't share the load during group projects because I don't trust my partners to do it right.

And sometimes, I won't take a leap of faith because I don't trust that God is leading me. I can't praise in the midst of my struggles because I don't really trust that God is good. I can't even receive grace because I don't trust that God is willing to give it to me, broken as I am.

Can you relate? No matter how many times we're told to trust in the Lord and no matter how often we read verses about God's goodness, faithfulness, and devotion to His children, we've still got some major trust issues. Whether in big ways or small, we avoid the sky-high tightrope of real, God-focused faith in favor of the ground level of nominal obedience. We sing praises to a trustworthy God but we hold our hearts close to home, not ever ready to let Him hold us because we worry He'll let us go.

It all begs the question: what's the solution to our trust issues? It can't be a giant leap into the unknown, because we can barely take small steps in confidence. How do we walk in new levels of trust when we're blind to the destination? Even now, I'm a little scared. Sure, I want to trust God more, but what does that really entail?

Well, whatever the journey is that God's about to take us on, we're in this together. All we can do is look to someone who sets the very best example, all of the time. Jesus trusted God like no one else. Maybe if we look to Him, we can learn to do the same. Ready? Let's go.

BEAUTIFUL KINGDOM

STOP AND PRAY!

> LORD, I WANT TO TRUST YOU MORE. PLEASE SHOW ME HOW AND STRENGTHEN ME AS I STEP INTO THE UNKNOWN.

This week we're going to read what is absolutely and without a doubt the hardest portion of Scripture in the whole Bible. It's the very darkest moment in history, the climax to Jesus's story that none of His friends saw coming. We're about to be witnesses to the suffering and death of Jesus. What better place to learn trust than from its biggest test? Jesus trusted God and walked humbly toward death on a cross. It's terrible, shocking, heart-breaking, and, somehow, *beautiful*.

Let's start in the Garden of Gethsemane. Read Matthew 26:36–46.

1. TRUST HIS PLAN.

09 / BEAUTIFUL TRUST

In the past, when I've studied this moment from the Bible, I've focused on the disciples. I've heard so many sermons about their sleepy tendencies while Jesus asked them to stay up and pray. It's a great message about being alert in prayer! But in this season, in light of the cross, the disciples feel very much like side characters. This story is about Jesus. And what's Jesus up to in this passage? He's suffering.

+ FILL IN THE BLANKS FROM MATTHEW 26:36–37.

"THEN JESUS WENT WITH HIS DISCIPLES TO A PLACE CALLED GETHSEMANE, AND HE SAID TO THEM, 'SIT HERE WHILE I GO OVER THERE AND PRAY.' HE TOOK PETER AND THE TWO SONS OF ZEBEDEE ALONG WITH HIM, AND HE BEGAN TO BE _____ AND _____."

After the Last Supper (the moment we learned about last week), Jesus headed up to an olive grove with His disciples for some time in prayer. Even though His friends were oblivious, Jesus knew that His time had come. Torture and death were fast approaching, and He needed time with His Father. In deep anguish (sweating drops of blood according to Luke), He prayed three times, shocking us with the contents of His prayer. He actually asked God to change His mind.

> **"GOING A LITTLE FARTHER, HE FELL WITH HIS FACE TO THE GROUND AND PRAYED, 'MY FATHER, IF IT IS POSSIBLE, MAY THIS CUP BE TAKEN FROM ME. YET NOT AS I WILL, BUT AS YOU WILL.'"**
> **Matthew 26:39**

BEAUTIFUL KINGDOM

Reading this, I'm struck by the utter humanity of Jesus. We know He is the Son of God, perfect in every way, but He still found Himself crying out to God when faced with His hardest calling. He knew what He had to do—His mission here on Earth—and He knew the outcome (spoiler: resurrection is coming!). But still, He wondered if God would change His mind. He begged for another way. Without sin, He felt all the feelings any person would when walking to their death.

Most of us know the verse that says Jesus sympathizes with all of our weaknesses (Hebrews 4:15), but this moment in the garden takes it to a whole new level. You probably haven't had to face death on a cross, but can you relate to Jesus here?

Think about the season of sickness that caused you to doubt if God would ever come through for you.

Think about the awful breakup you went through with the guy you thought was your husband that filled you with shame for giving your heart away to the wrong person.

Think about the loss of your loved one, when you fell so deep into sorrow you wondered if you'd ever feel happy again.

Did you beg the Lord to take the pain away? Did you pray for circumstances to change? Did you cry? *So did Jesus.* We are going to face sorrow, pain, and struggle in our lives. You're not wrong to cry out! You're not wrong to ask God to rescue you from your situation! But we can learn something crucial from Jesus's struggle: He trusted God's plan in the midst of it.

"YET NOT AS I WILL, BUT AS YOU WILL."
Matthew 26:39b

09 / BEAUTIFUL TRUST

Right there in the middle of what may have been the hardest moment of His life up to that point, and while He asked God to change it, He still submitted to the Father's plan. He still trusted that God knew what He was doing. Maybe we can learn something from that! What if we don't have to wait until our circumstances are better to believe that God is good? What if instead, we can step into trust right in the middle of the storm? We can trust that God, who can see the bigger picture, has a plan for His glory and for our good.

If you're in the midst of a season of suffering right now and you're crying out to God, I believe that trust can start right here. We can look up at our Father, just like Jesus did, and say, *Your will be done*.

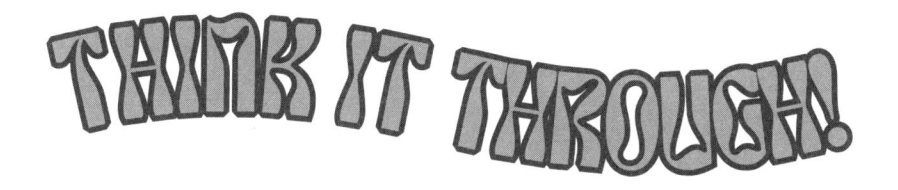

THINK IT THROUGH!

+ WHAT MOMENT OR SEASON IN YOUR OWN LIFE COMES TO MIND WHEN YOU READ THIS PORTION OF SCRIPTURE?

BEAUTIFUL KINGDOM

+ DID YOU STRUGGLE TO TRUST GOD'S PLAN IN THE MIDST OF IT? WHY OR WHY NOT?

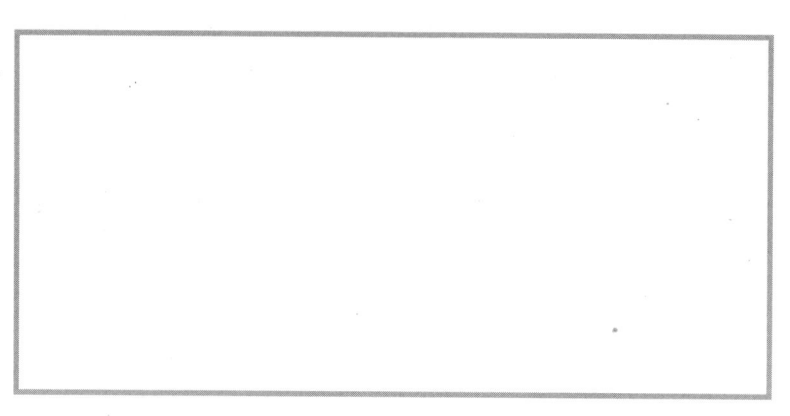

```
┌─────────────────────────────────────────┐
│                                         │
│                                         │
│                                         │
│                                         │
│                                         │
└─────────────────────────────────────────┘
```

These are baby steps to beautiful trust as modeled by Jesus. First, we learn to trust His plan. Next, we learn to trust His presence.

2. TRUST HIS PRESENCE.

Read Matthew 27:32–49.

Note: this is a hard read, so take your time and invite God into it!

One year at church camp when I was in high school, I remember sitting in a bunk with a few other girls as my youth group leader told the story of Jesus's death and resurrection. Really, she was presenting the gospel to us, even if we didn't know it at the time. And when she got to the part about Jesus dying for our sins, she started crying.

I was caught off guard. I had grown up in church, been to a million Good Friday and Easter services, and watched *The Passion of the Christ* at way too young an age. So I was familiar with the story of the crucifixion. But never in my life had I heard someone *cry* when talking about it. That leader knew an intimacy with Jesus I hadn't even begun to delve into in my own faith walk. His suffering was hers. His death was personal for her.

09 / BEAUTIFUL TRUST

I wonder if we could allow that same tenderness to flood our hearts as we read these verses. Don't let your heart grow callous to the story of Jesus's death. It really happened; it was brutal, terrible, and heart-wrenching. Let yourself feel the weight of it! Because He did it for *you*.

+ WHAT STANDS OUT TO YOU OR HITS YOUR HEART THE MOST FROM MATTHEW 27:32–49?

For me, one of the most striking parts of Jesus's crucifixion story (though it's certainly all striking) lies in verse 46.

> **"ABOUT THREE IN THE AFTERNOON JESUS CRIED OUT IN A LOUD VOICE, 'ELI, ELI, LEMA SABACHTHANI?' (WHICH MEANS 'MY GOD, MY GOD, WHY HAVE YOU FORSAKEN ME?')."**
> Matthew 27:46

If you're a Bible nerd, this verse is a gold mine. Jesus is actually quoting Scripture here! (It comes from Psalm 22.) It's also so cool that the Biblical authors wrote it down in Aramaic, the common tongue of the ancient Near East. It really helps us understand the fervor with which Jesus was crying out.

But when we stop to think about what He's saying, it hits like a punch to the gut. Jesus, the One with the most intimate connection to the Father, was in despair because His Father, God Almighty, had turned away. Utterly forsaken.

BEAUTIFUL KINGDOM

Shocking, right? What's going on here?

At this moment, a holy transaction took place. God the Father regarded God the Son as if He were a sinner. Paul explains it this way, that *God made him who had no sin to be sin for us, so that in him we might become the righteousness of God* (2 Corinthians 5:21). For us, Jesus had to endure as God turned His face from Him and allowed His wrath to pour on Him. Horrible as it was, it fulfilled God's good and loving plan for redemption—the plan that's been unfolding all throughout the Bible. Yes, God had to turn away from His Son at that moment, but He didn't stay away. 2 Corinthians tells us that on the cross, God was reconciling the world back to Him in Christ.[1]

> "THEREFORE, IF ANYONE IS IN CHRIST, THE NEW CREATION HAS COME: THE OLD HAS GONE, THE NEW IS HERE! ALL THIS IS FROM GOD, WHO RECONCILED US TO HIMSELF THROUGH CHRIST AND GAVE US THE MINISTRY OF RECONCILIATION: THAT GOD WAS RECONCILING THE WORLD TO HIMSELF IN CHRIST, NOT COUNTING PEOPLE'S SINS AGAINST THEM."
> 2 Corinthians 5:17–19

So, where does the trust come in? We know that Jesus trusted God's plan enough to go to the cross. But the wild thing is that He stayed on the cross even when God had to turn away. When He couldn't feel the presence, when nobody was there to remind Him, He still trusted God.

I don't know about you, but trusting God is so much easier for me when I feel Him moving. I can more easily take a step out in faith when I've seen ten different signs pointing me on the way. I can more easily trust that God is real when I get goose bumps from His

09 / BEAUTIFUL TRUST

presence at a worship night. But the second I don't feel Him, when I can't see with my eyes that He's there, or when the going gets tough, trust begins to feel impossible.

If you've been walking with the Lord for any period of time, you'll know that there are seasons when He feels close and seasons when He feels far. But if we are following Jesus's example, it means that we are called to trust the Lord even when it's hard—even when we don't feel Him. We have to trust that He will never leave us or forsake us, like His Word says. We have to trust that the intimate relationship with our God that Jesus bought for us on the cross is enough.

Even when we don't feel it, we trust that God is with us, working all things together for our good. We trust His holy, consistent, wrap-around presence.

+ HAVE YOU EVER HAD TO TRUST GOD EVEN WHEN YOU COULDN'T FEEL HIM THERE? WHAT WAS IT LIKE?

We've begun to trust God's good plan and His consistent presence, so what's left? Now, we learn to trust the ending.

BEAUTIFUL KINGDOM

3. TRUST THE ENDING.

Read Matthew 27:50–61.

If you ever doubted that the Bible is real, that all of this actually happened, then this portion of Scripture proves it to you. Because if you were trying to make up a convincing story about a Savior God who was coming to rescue His people, you wouldn't have Him die a public and torturous death right as He was hitting a stride in His ministry. This right here, the crucifixion, is the very image of the unexpected, beautiful Kingdom. No matter how many times Jesus warned us, no matter how often the Hebrew Scripture foretold it, it's still shocking.

After all that, Jesus *died*.

> **"AND WHEN JESUS HAD CRIED OUT AGAIN IN A LOUD VOICE, HE GAVE UP HIS SPIRIT."**
> **Matthew 27:50**

His friends had to bury Him in a stranger's tomb. Jesus, their Messiah, dead in a grave. It's depressing, right? We can't even imagine what the disciples were thinking, how defeated and utterly devastated they must have felt.

But thousands of years later, we don't feel the same devastation when we read this. We don't look at the story and see defeat. In fact, we celebrate this moment. Why? *Because we know the ending!*

Jesus didn't stay dead! On the cross, He bore the weight of our sins, proclaiming victory over sin and death. On the third day, He rose again, inviting all who would believe in Him into eternal life. That's the good news! That's the joy set before Jesus (Hebrews 12:2)! That's how He could walk boldly toward the cross, because

09 / BEAUTIFUL TRUST

He trusted God's good plan. He trusted the ending, that He would get to reconcile all of His lost sheep back to Himself!

Maybe that's what trust in God really boils down to: knowing the end. Knowing that one day, we're going to live in paradise with Him, in His house where He's already prepared us a room. It's believing that one day, Jesus is returning to make a new Heaven and a new Earth. It's trusting that God isn't going to leave us hanging, that our stories aren't going to end in tragedy, and that our good God is calling us home to Him.

I love how these verses from 2 Corinthians describe this beautiful trust in the ending:

> "THEREFORE WE DO NOT LOSE HEART. THOUGH OUTWARDLY WE ARE WASTING AWAY, YET INWARDLY WE ARE BEING RENEWED DAY BY DAY. FOR OUR LIGHT AND MOMENTARY TROUBLES ARE ACHIEVING FOR US AN ETERNAL GLORY THAT FAR OUTWEIGHS THEM ALL. SO WE FIX OUR EYES NOT ON WHAT IS SEEN, BUT ON WHAT IS UNSEEN, SINCE WHAT IS SEEN IS TEMPORARY, BUT WHAT IS UNSEEN IS ETERNAL."
> **2 Corinthians 4:16–18, emphasis added**

Doesn't this get you so hyped up!? Our God has adopted us into His family and promised us eternal life with Him! How can we struggle with trusting Him when we fix our eyes on Heaven?

Ladies, *this is the beautiful Kingdom! This is the good news of the gospel!* God has good plans for you, here on Earth and in Heaven.

BEAUTIFUL KINGDOM

He resurrected Jesus from the dead! Why can't we trust that He'll come through for us? He can resurrect your heart from that season of depression. He can resurrect your faith in your season of doubt. He can resurrect your health when your body fails you. He can even remind you of His presence in the midst of the suffering you're facing. And, one day, we get to sit down at the dinner table with Him, face-to-face.

It's so clear. Can you feel it settling in your spirit, seeping life into your dry bones? Trust issues cannot stand in the face of a good God who crossed the universe to win your heart. This week, allow God to hold your hand as you take baby steps toward trusting the Father like Jesus does.

The journey might be hard, but the destination is great.

09 / BEAUTIFUL TRUST

BEAUTIFUL KINGDOM

CONVERSATION STARTERS

1. What's your history with the crucifixion story? How does reading about Jesus's death make you feel (numb, sad, overwhelmed, confused)?

2. Look back at Jesus's prayers in the Garden of Gethsemane. What can you learn from the way Jesus cried out to the Father?

09 / **BEAUTIFUL TRUST**

3. It's hard to trust God when we don't feel Him there. Where in your life currently does God feel far? How can you step into deeper trust through that circumstance?

4. Jesus is preparing a place for us in Heaven! How can you let that hope for eternity affect your everyday life?

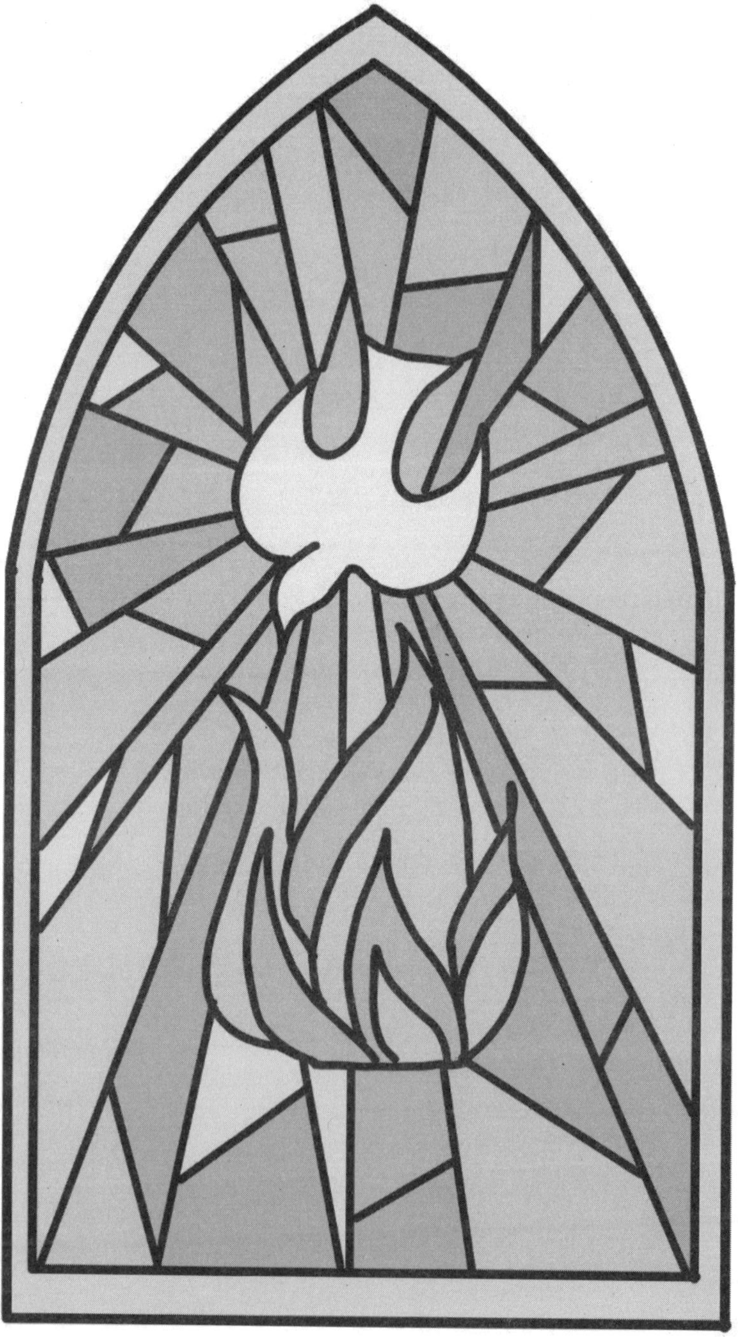

Women on Mission

CHAPTER 10

BEAUTIFUL KINGDOM

Women on Mission

Matthew 28

I don't know about you, but I'm feeling grateful this week. We just got to spend ten weeks hanging out with Jesus, our Savior. We got to learn from His Word, encounter Him in new ways, and catch glimpses of the beauty of the Kingdom of Heaven. We got to study His story and fall more in love with His character. I am overwhelmed with gratitude! What a privilege it is to be in the presence of a beautiful King!

But, as grateful as I am, I'm also feeling a little bit sentimental. Because we've finally arrived at the end. Chapter 10. The finale of our Matthew adventure. (Cue the tears!)

This chapter is going to be an exciting one, especially after the cliff-hanger from last week. We finally get to read about the resurrection! And I think that as you read, you'll discover something about the story that's pretty cool . . .

According to Matthew, the resurrection is kinda *girly*.

10 / WOMEN ON MISSION

Don't believe me? Read it for yourself! Take a few minutes and read Matthew 28.

+ SUMMARIZE MATTHEW 28 IN YOUR OWN WORDS.

This week, we're going to celebrate the resurrection of Jesus Christ! Thank you, Lord, for raising your Son from the dead! Thank you, Jesus, for winning the victory over sin and death! I mean, if any chapter of the Bible should lead you to have a praise party, this one is it.

And on top of that, we're going to take a look at the women who were integral to the story we read in Matthew 28. It's so crazy that women play such an important role in the most important part of the story of Jesus! We're going to learn from their example as we praise Jesus right alongside them.

Did you know that as a woman, you have a critical part to play in the Kingdom of Heaven? Have you embraced that calling on your life? Are you a woman on mission for Jesus?

Confession time: Growing up, I was the opposite of a girly girl. Even into high school, I despised the color pink, thought sparkles were lame, and avoided women's gatherings at my church like they were the plague.

I know, I know. It's super ironic because I now work for a women's ministry and wear pink almost exclusively. But I think when I was younger, I was almost embarrassed to be a girl. I thought girly-ness made me weak, and I wanted to be strong like I thought the boys were. But now when I read the Bible, I'm struck by the unique power God has given us as women.

I think about Deborah in the book of Judges and how she heard the Lord's voice. I think of the radical obedience of Ruth. I think of the love of Mary, the mother of Jesus. I think of Mary of Bethany and her intimate friendship with Jesus. I think of Priscilla, who's mentioned in Acts, Romans, 1 Corinthians, *and* 2 Timothy—Priscilla, the discipler.

When we read the Bible, we see so many strong women sold out for what God called them to do. Girly-ness and pink and sparkles aside, I believe that God has a unique calling on our lives as women, a calling we love to celebrate as a women's ministry (though we love and honor the men, too!). My prayer is that you would feel empowered and inspired to step out and live as a woman on mission for Jesus.

Let's look back at the story of Jesus's death and resurrection and see what the women were up to.

+ FLIP TO MATTHEW 27:55–56. WHAT WOMEN WERE MENTIONED HERE? WHAT WERE THEY DOING?

+ NOW, CHECK OUT MATTHEW 27:61. WHICH WOMEN WERE MENTIONED HERE? WHAT WERE THEY DOING?

10 / WOMEN ON MISSION

+ LASTLY, COPY DOWN MATTHEW 28:1 IN THE SPACE BELOW.

[ ]

The first thing we can learn from the women surrounding Jesus at the resurrection, according to Matthew 28:1, is that they were *bold*.

1. THE WOMEN WERE BOLD.

To get some context for this, we're going to need to check the other Gospel accounts of the events surrounding Jesus's death and resurrection. Remember, Matthew, Mark, Luke, and John (the first four books of the New Testament) tell the same story of Jesus from different vantage points, offering unique perspectives and different details. When you piece the accounts together, you learn that the eleven disciples (minus Judas) actually spent the days following Jesus's death in hiding because they feared the very real and very present backlash of the Jewish authorities. Check it out!

> "ON THE EVENING OF THAT FIRST DAY OF THE WEEK, WHEN THE DISCIPLES WERE TOGETHER, <u>WITH THE DOORS LOCKED FOR FEAR OF THE JEWISH LEADERS,</u> JESUS CAME AND STOOD AMONG THEM AND SAID, 'PEACE BE WITH YOU!'"
> John 20:19, emphasis added

We can't even imagine what these critical days were like, the pressure all of Jesus's friends were under and the confusion and fear that must have been overwhelming. The Scripture tells us that, understandably, the disciples had varying reactions to the events surrounding the crucifixion. At Jesus's arrest, every single one of them—His closest friends—had scattered and run for the hills (Matthew 26:56). Peter went off to a courtyard to deny he even knew Jesus (Matthew 26:69–75), and one account even says that the disciple John was the only one of the twelve who was present as Jesus breathed His last breath (John 19:26).

It makes sense! I think most of us would have reacted in similar ways. But, amazingly—according to Matthew's account—there were actually friends of Jesus who stuck it out with Him to the end.

> **"MANY WOMEN WERE THERE, WATCHING FROM A DISTANCE. THEY HAD FOLLOWED JESUS FROM GALILEE TO CARE FOR HIS NEEDS. AMONG THEM WERE MARY MAGDALENE, MARY THE MOTHER OF JAMES AND JOSEPH, AND THE MOTHER OF ZEBEDEE'S SONS."**
> Matthew 27:55–56

These women were bold enough to stand in the face of brutal death to be with Jesus in His darkest moments. When so many found themselves running, it was these few women who stood by Him, caring for His needs as He was marched toward death on a cross. It was two women (Mary Magdalene and Mary, the mother of James) who came to His tomb and were the very first witnesses to the resurrection (Matthew 28:1).

I get goose bumps just reading these verses. Women—friends and followers of Jesus—walked alongside Him. Women got to be

10 / WOMEN ON MISSION

the very first people to hear of the resurrection, the most exciting moment in all of history. What an honor! What a privilege! How can we read that and not take it personally? As women of God, we are called to be bold, and, through that boldness, we get to stand witness to glorious moves of God.

Most of us will never have to stand by a friend as they die, and most of us have never brought spices to a tomb before. But we all have opportunities in our day-to-day lives to be bold for Jesus. Boldness is stepping out when it's uncomfortable. It means relying on courage that comes from God in the face of fear. It means shameless, unafraid commitment to the Lord in face of resistance.

You're invited to boldness when you pray over a friend who is having a hard time. You're invited to boldness when you share the good news of Jesus with a stranger. You're invited to boldness when you start up a conversation with the girl at Bible study who looks lonely. In every instance, you are stepping closer to Jesus. In communion with Him, you are bearing witness to the cross, just like the women who came before you.

+ CAN YOU THINK OF A TIME WHEN YOU HAD TO PUSH THROUGH DISCOMFORT OR FEAR TO BE BOLD FOR JESUS? DESCRIBE IT BELOW.

Now, finally, we get to explore the very best moment in the whole Bible: Jesus's resurrection. And we get to learn from the women who received the message.

BEAUTIFUL KINGDOM

Reread Matthew 28:1–10.

+ WHICH PART OF THIS PASSAGE STANDS OUT TO YOU THE MOST? WHY?

The significance of this Easter-morning moment cannot be overstated. Jesus Christ, Son of God, died in our place to rescue us from our sins. Then, on the third day, He rose again, claiming eternal victory over sin and death and inviting all of us to spend eternity with Him in Heaven. Praise God! Hallelujah!

CONTEXT!
Mary Magdalene is a woman who Jesus healed from a pretty severe demon infestation. She was a committed follower of Jesus, popping up all over His story. The other Mary was the mother of James, one of Jesus's disciples.

In line with the way He usually ushered in the Kingdom, the announcement of the resurrection was pretty awesome. There was an earthquake, the stone in front of the tomb rolled away, and an angel who looked like *lightning* (yes, lightning) appeared to chat with Mary and Mary.

"THE ANGEL SAID TO THE WOMEN, 'DO NOT BE AFRAID, FOR I KNOW THAT YOU ARE LOOKING FOR JESUS, WHO WAS CRUCIFIED. HE IS NOT HERE; HE HAS RISEN, JUST AS HE SAID. COME AND SEE THE PLACE WHERE HE LAY. THEN GO QUICKLY AND TELL HIS DISCIPLES: 'HE HAS RISEN FROM THE DEAD AND IS GOING AHEAD OF YOU INTO GALILEE. THERE YOU WILL SEE HIM.' NOW I HAVE TOLD YOU."

Matthew 28:5-7

10 / WOMEN ON MISSION

The lightning-like angel announced to Mary and Mary that Jesus had risen. Then, he told them to spread the word.

2. THE WOMEN WERE GIVEN A MESSAGE.

My friend recently got engaged in front of the Eiffel Tower (dreamy, I know). I had been a part of their story leading up to the happy moment, watching as she sent her boyfriend ring ideas and as she dreamed with me about possible wedding venues. But she didn't know *when* he was going to propose.

But I knew.

I remember getting dinner with her the night before they left for Paris, bursting with excitement for what I knew was going to be a life-changing adventure. I could barely contain my joy—anticipation of the secret finally being revealed was killing me. I had this huge news, the best secret ever, right on the tip of my tongue. I couldn't wait to celebrate with her! It was almost impossible to keep it in.

I wonder if that's how Mary and Mary felt after the angel gave them the message. Scripture says they "hurried" away from the tomb, "afraid yet filled with joy." I can imagine the smiles on their faces, the tears in their eyes. I just know their hearts were beating so fast, excited to share the best news of their lives. *Jesus has risen*.

Then, on their way, they ran into Jesus Himself (Matthew 28:8–10). What a moment! They collapsed at His feet, worshiping Him with joy. And He, just like the angel, told them to share the message.

Did you know that you've been given a message, too? As a daughter of the King, adopted into the family of Jesus by His blood, you have this amazing news in your heart—the best message right on the tip of your tongue. You were given the good news of the resurrection, just like Mary and Mary were.

But are you hurrying off to share it?

I think so often we get used to the joy of life with Jesus. It feels so normal that we lose the bubbling-up excitement to share the message with the people around us. Let this Scripture reinvigorate you! You, as a woman of God, have a unique message that only you can share. Only you can tell the story of how Jesus met you in your darkest moments. Only you can share the intimacy of what the cross means to you. Only you can share the joy that life with Jesus has brought you.

Your story, the message Jesus has given you by the wonder of His resurrection, matters. And only you can tell it.

> "HOW BEAUTIFUL ON THE MOUNTAINS ARE THE FEET OF THOSE WHO BRING GOOD NEWS, WHO PROCLAIM PEACE, WHO BRING GOOD TIDINGS, WHO PROCLAIM SALVATION, WHO SAY TO ZION, 'YOUR GOD REIGNS!'"
> **Isaiah 52:7**

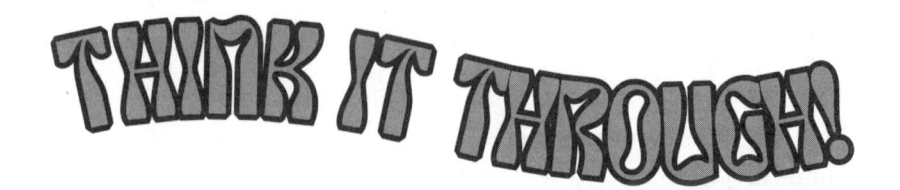

THINK IT THROUGH!

+ TAKE THIS OPPORTUNITY TO REMIND YOURSELF OF THE GOOD NEWS OF JESUS. WHAT'S YOUR STORY? HOW

10 / WOMEN ON MISSION

HAS HE MOVED IN YOUR LIFE? WHAT DOES THE CROSS MEAN TO YOU? WRITE YOUR "MESSAGE" IN THE SPACE BELOW!

+ HAS THE JOY OF THE MESSAGE STARTED TO GROW OLD FOR YOU? TAKE A MOMENT TO PRAY. ASK GOD TO GIVE YOU NEW JOY FOR HIS STORY. RECORD YOUR PRAYERS BELOW.

BEAUTIFUL KINGDOM

Somehow, we've reached the end of Matthew's Gospel. I'm fascinated by the way he leaves it, what he records as the last words of Jesus here on earth—the last imperative from our Savior. It's known as the Great Commission.

Reread Matthew 28:16–20.

Mary and Mary's message had reached them, and the disciples made their way to Galilee to meet with the risen Jesus. When He appeared before them, they worshiped Him. Though, sadly, some doubted. Then, before He ascended into Heaven to sit at the right hand of the Father, Jesus left them with one last challenge.

+ COPY DOWN THE GREAT COMMISSION FROM MATTHEW 28:19–20 IN THE SPACE BELOW.

After ushering in the beautiful Kingdom in miraculous, shocking, and heart-breaking ways, Jesus had one thing left to say: *go*.

3. WE ARE ALL SENT.

There's this moment all the way back in the book of Isaiah that I can't get out of my head as I read the Great Commission. Isaiah the prophet was in the throne room of God having a pretty crazy experience. (Go back and read all of Isaiah 6 in your own time. So cool!) There, God commissioned him, too.

10 / WOMEN ON MISSION

+ FILL IN THE BLANKS FROM ISAIAH 6:8.

"THEN I HEARD THE VOICE OF THE LORD SAYING, 'WHOM SHALL I SEND? AND WHO WILL GO FOR US?' AND I SAID, 'HERE AM I. _____ _____!'"

You and I weren't there on the mountain during the Great Commission. But I wonder how we would have responded. Would we have listened, but doubted? Would we have felt a temporary high, then given up when it got hard? Or would we have said, just as Isaiah did, all those years before, *Here I am. Send me!*

You see, we are all sent. The Great Commission is just as much for us as it was for the original hearers. We are all charged to look God in the eyes and say, *Here I am. Send me!*

What's He sending us to do? Well, according to Matthew 28, we are being sent to make disciples, baptize, and teach. We're called to reach out to the whole world, inviting them into a relationship with Jesus. We're called to baptize them into the family of God, calling on the name of the Father, the Son, and the Holy Spirit. We're called to teach everyone what we've been taught, to look to Jesus and to learn from Him.

Who are we being sent to? Just as Jesus was, we're sent to the lost. In every nation, we are called to seek and save the lost. God desires every single person to know Him. And He's doing that through you and me. *Here I am. Send me!*

This Scripture is an invitation. Jesus is inviting you to *go*. To go all in, to go all out, and to go wherever He calls. He's inviting you to find people on your campus who are lost. You can share the good news of Jesus with them. He's inviting you to be the hands and feet of Jesus to the needy, showing them what it looks like to live for something greater than yourself. He's inviting you to be bold, stepping out when your comfort zone wants you to stay in.

BEAUTIFUL KINGDOM

Here I am. Send me!

And the best part is we don't have to do it alone! We get to link arms with other women of God who share the very same calling. We are women on mission for Jesus, together. Your small group, your Delight chapter, your church community, your city. You are called to run together, eagerly sharing the best news ever: the invitation into life with Jesus.

Are you hyped up? We're ready to run, to go where we're called to go. We've seen how God has moved in our lives, and we want to invite every single person to experience the same thing. Armed with the knowledge of Scripture (look at how well you know Matthew now!) and blessed with an intimacy with your Savior, you are sent. So the only thing left to do is go.

Here we are. Send us.

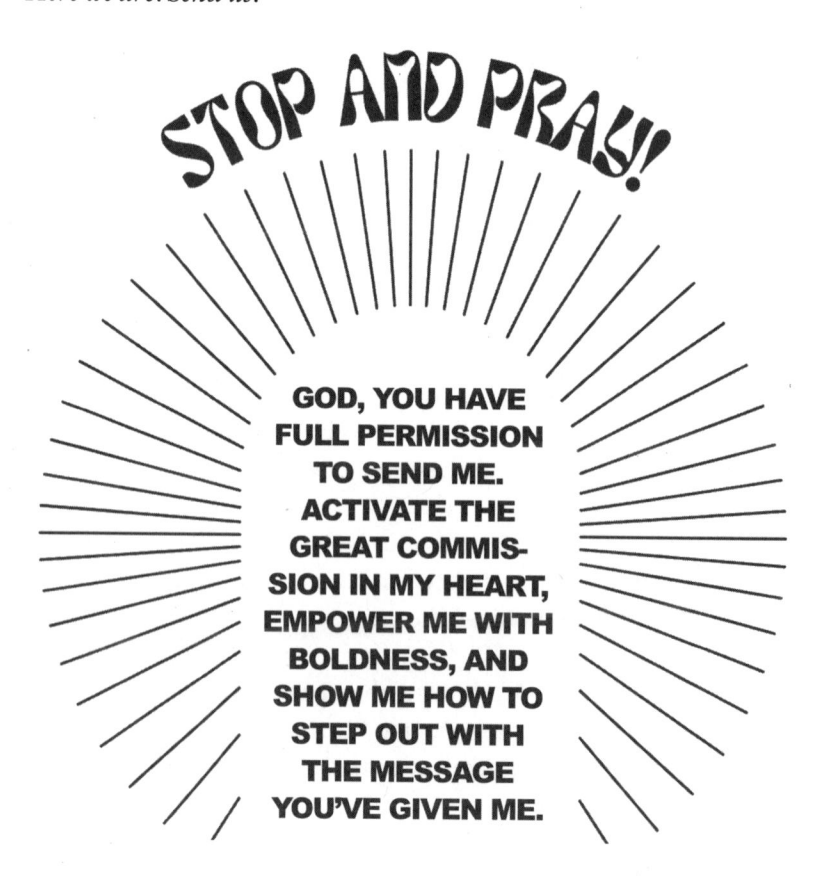

STOP AND PRAY!

GOD, YOU HAVE FULL PERMISSION TO SEND ME. ACTIVATE THE GREAT COMMISSION IN MY HEART, EMPOWER ME WITH BOLDNESS, AND SHOW ME HOW TO STEP OUT WITH THE MESSAGE YOU'VE GIVEN ME.

10 / WOMEN ON MISSION

CONVERSATION STARTERS

1. The women at the tomb hurried off to share the good news of the resurrection. Be honest... Are you in the same hurry? Do you feel an urgency to share the Gospel? Why or why not?

2. In the Think It Through section, we brainstormed our personal "messages." Now that you have your story of how Jesus moved in your life, how do you feel called to share it? Is there someone you know who might be encouraged by your story?

10 / WOMEN ON MISSION

3. How has your relationship with Jesus grown, changed, or matured throughout our Matthew study? What was your biggest takeaway?

4. We just spent ten weeks exploring the beautiful Kingdom Jesus came to announce. Which aspect of the Kingdom stood out to you the most that you want to take with you into this next season? Write it out, then praise God for it!

ABOUT THE AUTHOR

HEY! I'M MAGGIE!

I am working my *dream job* as Curriculum Development Coordinator here at Delight Ministries. I like to think of myself as Delight's translator. My job is to take God's powerful, perfect, and active Word and present it to college women in a way that helps them see how relevant it is for their own lives... *AND I LOVE IT!*

On the weekends, catch me serving in my church's kids ministry with my husband and eating a lot of microwave popcorn. I love to read, I'm a die-hard Swiftie, and I'll never say no to a *Twilight* marathon.

CONTRIBUTORS

EDITING TEAM:

Theological Editing by Aubrey Johnston
Editing by Maddie Grimes

DESIGN:

Hailey Sheppard

SPECIAL THANKS TO . . .

Abigail Pace, Brittney Clay, Carly Renbarger, Emily Iniesta, Emma Petno, Gbemi Abon, Isabelle Jarvis, Julia Miller, Julianna Hardesty, Malayna Eudy, Taylor McCutcheon, Trinity Romesberg, Hannah Rady, Maddie Middleton

NOTES

02 | CHAPTER 2: HOW TO PRAY
1. Bertonini, Dewar, et al. *The Book of Matthew.* The Smart Guide to the Bible Series, Thomas Nelson, 2008, pp. 92.
2. Quarles, Charles L. "Matthew," in CSB Study Bible: Notes, ed. Edwin A. Blum and Trevin Wax (Nashville, TN: Holman Bible Publishers, 2017), 1509.

04 | CHAPTER 4: JESUS AND MESSY PEOPLE
1. Gizik, David. *Matthew: Verse by Verse Commentary*, "Matthew 3—Healing, Teaching, and Miracles," Enduring Word, 2019, pp. 123.
2. Ortlund, Dane. *Gentle and Lowly: The Heart of Christ for Sinners and Sufferers.* "Chapter 2: His Heart in Action," Crossway, 2018, pp. 30.

08 | CHAPTER 8: FOR THE LEAST OF THESE
1. "Parables." *Dictionary.com*, Houghton Mifflin Harcourt Publishing Company, 2005, *https://www.dictionary.com/browse/Parables*.

09 | CHAPTER 9: BEAUTIFUL TRUST
1. Gizik, David. *Matthew: Verse by Verse Commentary*, Enduring Word, 2019, pps. 424–425.

START A DELIGHT

HELP US SPREAD THE WORD ABOUT DELIGHT!

There are thousands of college women all across the country that need Christ-centered community but have no idea Delight exists!!! We need women like you to help spread the word.

If this community has impacted your life in any way, don't you want to help other women experience it, too?

If you know a friend who loves Jesus and who would make an amazing Delight leader—tell her about Delight! With just a few texts you could indirectly reach hundreds of college women on another campus!

How cool is that?!

www.delightministries.com

Point them to our website where they can sign up to bring Delight to their campus! Once they sign up, they will hear from us and will get everything they need to make this community happen at their university.

So . . . send a couple texts, call a couple friends, maybe post about it on your socials, and let's reach a million more college women together!

DELIGHT WORSHIP

It all started with a question . . . *What if we could write worship music for college women?*

SO WE DID! Delight Worship is intentional music created to connect college women to the heart of Jesus.

Listen today!

YEARBOOK PAGE

FILL THESE PAGES WITH SWEET NOTES FROM YOUR DELIGHT COMMUNITY!

For more information, resources, or encouragement head to . . .

www.delightministries.com